A Critical Study of

THE LIFE AND TEACHINGS
Of
SRI GURU NANAK DEV
THE FOUNDER OF SIKHISM

A Critical Study of

THE LIFE AND TEACHINGS

of

SRI GURU NANAK DEV

THE FOUNDER OF SIKHISM

SEWARAM SINGH THAPAR

White Falcon Publishing

www.whitefalconpublishing.com

A Critical Study of
The Life and Teachings
of
SRI GURU NANAK DEV
THE FOUNDER OF SIKHISM
Sewaram Singh Thapar

www.whitefalconpublishing.com

ISBN:- 978-93-89085-09-9

To
The Seeker After Truth

Servants of God! --- Or Sons
Shall I not call you? Because
Not as servants ye knew
Your father's innermost mind,
His, who unwillingly sees
One of his little one lost ------
Yours in the praise, If mankind
Hath not as yet in its march
Fainted and fallen and died!

Matthew Arnold

PREFACE

> When at first I took my pen in hand
> Thus for to write, I did not understand
> That I at all should make a little book
> In such a mode; any, I had undertook
> To make another; which, when almost done,
> Before I was aware I this begun.
>
> *Bunyan*

In offering to the public a volume on the life and teachings of Guru Nanak Dev, the founder of Sikhism, no customary apology is needed. The importance of Sikh History is being felt more and more keenly every day. Sikhism as one of *the religious systems of the world*, perhaps has the most recent origin and yet the remarkable progress which it made in the land of its birth within three short centuries is quite unique. The Western mind was first directed towards it when, more than half a century ago, the British Extended their frontier to the River Sutlej, beyond which existed a kingdom, till then unnoticed by the British occupiers of rest of India, but which the latter had to fight against in a short interval. In their contest with the Sikhs, the victorious, had to respectfully acknowledge the strength and zeal of their enemies and ever since the annexation of the kingdom of the Sikhs by the British, the khalsa have supplied soldiers to the British Army, who have been next to none in the world in soldierly qualities, which have been put to test not only in India and its borders but also in China, Africa and other foreign countries. It was with the objective of explaining what real Sikhism, in all its pristine glory at the time of its great Founder, was and how it gradually developed into a church militant, that this work was originally started. My idea in the beginning was to write a brief essay on the subject, but afterwards, its re-writing, on the suggestion of certain friends, resulted in the adoption of the bigger and by nature more permanent scheme.

The time and the labour which I had to spend on the preparation of this work have been enormous, as compared with my capacities. My only excuse in taking up the self- imposed task was in the fact that a good deal of misunderstanding prevailed regarding the origin and development of Khalsa Church. The work of Malcolm and McGregor and the excellent volume from the pen of Captain Cunningham on Sikh History does not afford much assistance in the solution of the point at issue, perhaps because these writers have devoted too little space to the so-to-say ancient history of Sikhs. They have mostly dealt with the political history of the Khalsa, which however does not really begin till after the demise of the Tenth and last of the Gurus. I have, therefore had to fall back upon the original sources, but here too the task was arduous. The History of the Sikh Gurus lies much in obscurity. The materials at our disposal are very chaotic and misleading. The authenticity of the few extant *Janamsakhis* (the biographies in vernacular of Guru Nanak), the original source of all present–day information about the life and work of the first Guru, has been seriously called in question. This much at any rate is certain that they cannot be accepted in their entirety as they stand. Many of them are full of mythological descriptions and fictitious tales. I need only point out regarding them that their use of necessity be very cautious. The most extant *Janamsakhi*, going under the title of *Bhai Bala's Janamsakhi*, exists in so many different versions that none appears to be quite authentic. Dr. Trump has the credit of unearthing an old manuscript *Janamsakhi,* in the India Office, London, which also though very brief and free from many later-day inventions, cannot be vouchsafed as perfectly correct. It was this huddle muddle sort of material that I had at my disposal. But the task, the more arduous it was the more worth attempting it appeared to me ; and the result I offer to the public, in the hope that it may be able to remove certain wrong notions which have hitherto been cherished about Guru Nanak and his work. Whether the critical public will be harsh on me or will look to my work leniently, I cannot say. But here, once for all, I ask the reader's indulgence, in as much as I have had to work during hours stolen from my daily task and the means at my disposal to make the book more thorough were rather scanty. I shall feel myself satisfied and amply remunerated if this little book serves the useful purpose of setting the movement for a closer research into the Life and Mission of Guru Nanak Dev agoing. I will be glad to correct any mistakes or supply any omissions, which may be pointed out to me, in the next edition, should it be called for.

In the last chapter I have not been able to resist the temptation of adopting certain expression from Renan's *Life of Christ*, as those expressions most fitly applied to the subject in hand. I therefore record here my grateful acknowledgements to the author of the said work.

Rawalpindi City
The 12th October 1904
S. S THAPAR

CONTENTS

CHAPTER 1

BIRTH AND TIMES

Nanak was born at Talwandi, now called Nankana Sahib, in the Lahore District, in November[1] 1469, of the Christian era. His father, *Mehta* Kalu, son of Shiv Ram Das, and mother, Tripta, were middle class Hindus of the Kshatriya caste and were much respected in their community. He was named after his sister, *Bibi* Nanki, who was so called as she was born in her *nanka*, the family abode of her maternal grand father.

The Afghans had established in the year 1459, at Delhi, the Lodhi dynasty of Sultans. "They," says Wheeler, in his Short History of India, "were bitter persecutors of the Hindus and their religion. They broke down temples and built mosques in their room, as in the days of Mahmud of Ghazni. A Brahman

---

1 One *Janamsakhi* of Guru Nanak fixes the date of his birth of 3rd of Baisakh, Sambat 1526, which date falls in the middle of April, 1469, and *Bhai* Gurdas also refers indirectly to the month of Baisakh (April). It is not quite certain as to which is the correct date. But I have adopted the one in November in the text for the reason that the fullmoon day of *Kartak pakhsh* which fluctuates from year to year in the month of November, and not the April day, is, to this day observed as Guru Nanak's birthday, wherever there are Sikhs in this province or elsewhere. The oldest *Janamsakhi* lying in the India Office, London, also refers to the April day, but if this be correct, there could be the reason for the Sikhs to have given it up, as if unanimously.

1

was put to death by a Sultan of this dynasty for maintaining that the religions of Hindus and Muhammadans were equally acceptable in the eyes of GOD.............................. The Afghans have left a bad name in India. Their passion for revenge has become a proverb. No man is said to be safe from the revenge of an elephant, a cobra, or an Afghan." Guru Nanak himself has described the political and religious atmosphere of the times when he was born, as follows:–

"Kings are butchers, cruelty is their knife and sense of duty has taken wings and vanished. Falsity prevails like the darkness of the darkest night, and the moon of truth is visible nowhere."[2]

Apart from the political anarchy and lawlessness prevailing under the Afghan rule, society was hopelessly divided in that period. Lawless Afghans had over-run the Hindustan, and were quite uncontrolled by Government. They were bitter enemies of Hindus, among whom they had settled and over whom they exercised great control. Each man did what was right in his own eyes, and whatever he could do with impunity appeared to him right. Widows and orphans could find no help against the powerful neighbours who divided their lands amongst themselves at their pleasure. The Hindus, on the other hand, were again hopelessly divided among themselves. Sunk low in the depth of ignorance and superstition, they had become spiritual slaves. It was a horrible sin, in the consequences of the rigid and stereotyped character of the caste system, for a Shudra to hear a Sanskrit *shlok*, which could only be adequately punished by pouring moulten lead into his ears. A Hindu could not associate with a Hindu and it was deemed an act of pollution to partake of food prepared by another Hindu, or to eat at the same table with him. Intermarriage was an institution not existing even in the domain of thought. Moreover, no man, under this system could make his position. His ambition could not be higher than

---

2   *Var* Majh, M. I *Shlok* 16(I)

ਕਲਿ ਕਾਤੀ ਰਾਜੇ ਕਾਸਾਈ, ਧਰਮ ਪੰਖ ਕਰਿ ਉਡ ਰਿਆ।
ਕੂੜੁ ਅਮਾਵਸ, ਸਚ ਚੰਦਰਮਾ, ਦੀਸੈ ਨਾਹੀ ਕਹਿ ਚੜਿਆ।

to follow the profession his father had followed and to work in it exactly on the same lines with them. No improved methods of work to be introduced. "Thus energy and life were fettered... Nature had for ever settled for him". "Into his caste a man was born, and bound to it for life, without regard to poverty or riches, talent, character or skills." "Human dignity and human feeling were bound up in separate castes, and political progress was impossible."[3] When the scions of the Afghan nobility settled among these Hindus, the latter were still more depressed and cowed down, and became social as bad as political, religious as bad as spiritual, slaves.

There was no less corruption among the religious systems which prevailed in the country during that period. Purity of heart and faith were no factors in the popular religious systems. Hinduism or Muhammadanism, both had become a set of formalities and ceremonies, which were performed by their votaries, as if, automatically. The root and object of these formalities were no longer understood. God was no longer an object of worship or faith. The Hindu, like the Hindu of the primitive times, worshipped the elements and various other gods and incarnations of God in various forms. And the Mussalman, with all his symbols and ceremonies, only deemed it necessary to attend at the Musjid to bow down in the "House of God," to repeat a certain set of Arabic words, without understanding or seeking to understand, their import, and to convert as many others to his pretended faith as he possibly could do with fair or foul, humane or inhumane, means. Otherwise, there were few honest religious men, with faith in heart, recognising none but God, although, like the Pharisee of old, people pretended to be righteous, religious and pious.[4]

---

3 Sanderwon's "Outlines of the History of the World".
4 This is how *Bhai* Gurdas has described, in his Vars, the religious confusion and hypocrisy which were prevailing at that time: —
  "19. There was quite a confusion in the world when four castes and as many ashrams got established. There were *Sannyasees* of ten different denominations, and the *Yogis* set up twelve paths. The

Nor, is it said, was the current of reform quite absent. The wave of religious revival had set in throughout India, and was not Brahmanical in its orthodoxy. This religious upheaval "was heterodox in its spirit of protest against forms and ceremonies and class distinctions based on birth, and ethical in its preferences of a pure heart, and of the law of love, to all other acquired merits and good works. This religious

---

Jangams and the *Jains* indulged in deceptions and disputes. The Brahmans in many ways set up contests between Shastras, Vedas and the Puranas. The six schools of philosophy were at daggers drawn and the thirty- six books added hypocrisy all around. The mystical and magical formule and alchemy had all got their faces blackened by miraculous pretensions. One was divided up into many and those in very horrible forms. Thus had all sunk low in superstition in this *Kali*yuga."

"20. Many ways were found in this world, and it was then that Mahommad also appeared. He took seventy-two tribes with him and spread enmity and jealousy all around. He set up fasts, and prayers and *eeds*, and bound the people with formalities. Then followed *Peers, Prophets*, and *Gouses* and Books, in many garbs. They pulled down temples and built mosques in their places. The heretics and others all fought against each other. Sin prevailed all around."

"21. Hindus have four castes and Mussalmans four sects. Selfishness, abuse, vanity and useless struggle rage (amongst them). Hindus have the Ganges and Benares and the Mussalmans have Kosha andn Mecca. Mussalmans take to circumcision, while Hindus are zealous for thread and mark on forehead. These call on Rama and those on Rahim, but the name is the same, and they are wandering in opposite ways. They have forgotten their *Vedas* and the *Qorans*, and the world is lost in avarice. Truth has remained aside and the Brahmans and *Mullah*s are dying in useless struggle. Thus the order of metempsychosis is not shaken off their heads."

"25 Then *Baba* came to holy places and public festivals; but all festivals and formalities were found useless in the absence of Love for, and Devotion to God. Brahma himself did not insist for Love, the Four *Vedas* and Smrities show this. Throughout the world, in the Satya, Treta, Dwapur and Kalli-yugas, all seems confusion, and the seeker after truth gets perplexed in so many formalities. God cannot be reached by hypocrisy. But absorption in The Shapeless and Formless One, the Faithful lose caste and wear humility. Then their labours are rewarded in the Kingdom of Heaven."

Var I.

revival was the work also of the people, of the masses and not of the classes. At its heads were saints, prophets, poets and philosophers," a few only of whom had passed before Nanak, and those too not in Punjab; though after him, followed a host of them here as elsewhere. The late Mr. Justice Ranade, from whose "Rise of the Maratha Power" the above quotation is taken, has devoted a full chapter of his book to this religious upheaval of the country, though he appears to have had scanty information about provinces other than the Maharashtra. "A few of these saints," says Mr. Ranade, "were women, a few more Mahomdan converts to Hinduism, nearly half of them were Brahmans, while there were representatives in the other half from among all the other castes, Marathas *kumbhis*, tailors, gardeners, potters, goldsmiths, repentant prostitutes, and slave girls, even the outcaste Mahars. Much of the interest of religious upheaval is centered in the facts we have noticed above, as they indicate plainly that the influence of higher spirituality was not confined to this or that class but permeated deep through all strata of society, male and female, high and low, literate and illiterate, Hindu or Mahomdan alike. These are features which the religious history of few other countries can match or reproduce, unless where the elevating influence is the result of a widespread popular awakening. In northern and eastern India a similar movement manifested itself, much at the same time. Nanak stirred up the Punjab to rise, and made a supreme effort to reconcile Hinduism and Mohamdanism. Chaitanya, in the far east, sought to bring men back from the worship of *shakti* and *kali* to the faith of Bhagvat, while Ramanand and Kabir, Tulsi Das and Sur Das, Jayadev and Rohi Das, contributed each in his own way to the work of spiritual enlightenment." It may here be pointed out that before Guru Nanak's birth[5], comparatively

---

5   Cheitan and Kabir, It may be noted, were Guru Nanak's contemporaries. Kabir was born before him; and Cheitan after being about 17 year younger than him. Guru Nanak is also shown to have visited Rav (Rohil) Das and Namdev at Bennres.

BIRTH AND TIMES

few of these saints flourished to make any substantial and lasting improvement in the masses, but the current of religious reform was, notwithstanding, there. Captain Cunningham compares them with Nanak as follows:–

"Thus, in the beginning of the sixteenth century, the Hindu mind was no longer stagnant or retrogressive; it had been leavened with Mahometanism and changed and quickened for a new development. Ramanand and Gorakh had preached religious equality and Cheitan had repeated that faith levelled caste; Kabir had denounced images and appealed to the people in their own tongue, and Vullubh had taught that effected devotion was consistent with the ordinary duties of the world. But these good and able men appear to have been so impressed with nothingness of this life that they deemed the amelioration of man's social condition as unworthy of a thought. They aimed chiefly at emancipation from priest-craft, or from the grossness of idolatry and polytheism. They formed pious associations of contented Quietists, or they gave themselves up to the contemplation of futurity in the hope of approaching bliss, rather than called upon their fellow creatures to throw aside every social as well as religious trammel and to arise a new people freed from the debasing corruption of ages. They perfected forms of dissent rather than planted the germs of nations, and their sects remain to this day as they left them. It was reserved for Nanak to perceive the true principles of reforms and to lay those broad foundations which enabled his successor Govind to fire the minds of his countrymen with a new nationality and to give practical effect to the doctrine that the lowest is equal with the highest, in race as in creed, in political rights as in religious hopes."

Such were the times when Guru Nanak took birth, and it was given to him to reform the society as he found it. Political lawlessness, social confusion, religious corruption, moral degradation and spiritual slavery: these were the order of the day and it was the most difficult task that could befall a man to raise the country from this hopeless condition. No doubt,

Ramanand, Gorakh and Kabir had already begun in Northern Hindustan to raise the people from their spiritual lethargy but as pointed out by Captain Cunningham, in the paragraph quoted above, these good men had not perceived the true principles of reform, which were needed under the circumstances. That Guru Nanak succeeded in bringing about the much needed reform, is sufficiently clear from the history of the Sikhs.

Legend says that, at the time of his birth, which had taken place at about 1 o'clock in the night, when the full moon was shining in all its glory, there were visible some super natural signs and the nurse was struck with the shining face of the baby. It is also said that the *Pundit* who was called by his father to draw his horoscope predicted his future greatness. Whatever credence may be given to these stories, we are at least sure that he showed signs in his very childhood of leading a spiritual life, and that, even if these stories be not believed to be wholly true, his followers were not slow to ascribe to him a divine origin and supernatural powers.

He did not mix freely with other children, and did not indulge in childish games with them. He seemed confident of his talents from the very beginning, and did not speak much. This led his parents once to think that he was not well. A physician was sent for and asked to diagnose his disease but nothing abnormal was found in his constitution.

There was then in those days a nobleman in Talwandi, Rai Bular by name, who was virtually the chief man in the village, and practically its master. Guru Nanak was yet in his early age when this Muhammadan grandee got a special liking from him, and Nanak found in him a patron and friend worthy of himself.

CB80

CHAPTER 2
EARLY LIFE

When still a boy of seven, all outward ceremonies, external appearances and worldly pursuits were hateful to Nanak, for they let people astray from the right path of *Bhakti*. Having been put by his father to the village school at that age, Nanak when given the first lesson, confronted his teacher with the question regarding the latter's own knowledge. The teacher was interested in the boy even before that time, and could not afford to offend the remarkable son of the village Patwari by giving him a lash or two, or even a rebuke, for the impertinent question, so he thought he had better amuse himself by talking with the lovely boy for a while. Hence he enumerated all the branches of learning which he had studied and all the characters which he could read and write. "But have you got the knowledge of God, O man?" said Nanak. "This thy learning will be of no avail to thee on the Day of Judgement. It pertains to the world and is acquired to get worldly enjoyments". After saying so, Guru Nanak proceeded to tell him what that knowledge was. "Learn, then, to renounce the earthly things, and let thy heart be filled with devotion to God, and with its aid let thy pure mind be constantly fixed on God, and this alone will save thee from punishment of thy sins."[6]

---

6 "Sri Rag M. 1 Sh. 6
ਜਾਲ ਮੋਹਿ, ਘਸ ਮਸ ਕਰ,
ਮਤ ਕਾਗਤ ਕਰ ਸਾਰ,

The teacher was struck with what he heard, and Nanak is said not to have attended school again. *Mehta* Kalu was disappointed and also somewhat indignant at the sudden close of Nanak's school career, but he was not very anxious about it, as he thought that the matters would certainly improve with years. At any rate, we find Nanak, is his ninth year, engaged in the business of pasturing cattle. It was one of those attempts which his father made to lead him into a worldly business. Nanak's habits of solitary meditation were probably interpreted by Kalu as his early propensities for fleeing from the company of men, and seeking that of the birds and animals of the jungle. And it was perhaps on this account that the occupation of pasturing cattle was selected for him. One day, he is stated to have gone a little far away with his cattle, and to have taken rest from the scorching rays of the midday Summer Sun under the shade of a tree. He had just stretched himself on the ground when sleep overcame him. Legend says that, so long as he was sleeping there, the shade of the particular tree did not move off his body, while the shadow of other trees continued moving with the advancing sun. It is, moreover, stated that a large cobra was

---

ਭਾਉ ਕਲਮ ਕਰ, ਚਿਤ ਲਿਖਾਰੀ,
  ਗੁਰ ਪੁਛ ਲਿਖ ਬੀਚਾਰ;
ਲਿਖ ਨਾਮ, ਸਲਾਹਿ ਲਿਖ,
  ਲਿਖ ਅੰਤ ਨ ਪਾਰਾਵਾਰ।
ਬਾਬਾ! ਇਹੁ ਲੇਖਾ ਲਿਖ ਜਾਣ,
  ਜਿਤ ਲੇਖੇ ਤਨ ਪੀੜੀਏ, ਤਿਥੇ ਹੋਵੇ ਸਚਾ ਨਿਸਾਣ।।

Its literal translation is a follows:-
"Burn attachment and dissolve it into ink, take the pure mind for paper, make Devotion thy pen and heart the writer, and write what the Guru tells thee: write the Name, write the Praise, write of the Endless and Limitless! *Baba!* Know to write this writing. Where thy body shall suffer for writings (records of sins), this shall be thy true beacon." Or, in other words, Let thy heart write on the paper of thy pure mind with the pen of devotion and ink of burnt attachment (of worldly things) the Name and praise of the Endless Being, and this will be thy true beacon where otherwise thou shall undergo torture on account of thy sins."

also sitting there with his hood spread like a canopy over his forehead. These were the days of appraisement of rent of lands, and Rai Bular, the grandee, was, therefore, out on his estate. When he was returning home, he witnessed the miraculous scene, and he as well as those with him were quite astonished with what they saw. Nanak was called from his sleep, and the cobra quietly left him. The Rai embraced and kissed Nanak. On reaching home he sent for Kalu, and having told him of all that he had seen, he warned him not to treat the boy harshly. But Kalu had just received complaints that the cattle under his son's watch were destroying the neighbouring crops. He expressed regret on account of these complaints which were now against told in the presence of the Rai. But "nay," says Nanak, "their crops *have not been destroyed*. Go and see if the crops be not just as they were." Rai Bular sent back the complainants to their farms, and, to their utter astonishment and mortification, they found the crops uninjured.

But Kalu, with his pecuniary propensities and worldly wisdom, could not be satisfied. He must try, as much as he could, to train his only son in *some* calling, in order to enable him to earn an independent living. His paternal heart could not rest while his son was proving a failure all around. After a period, which seems to have extended to some years, of constant anxieties, he put Nanak into agriculture. Nanak implicitly obeyed. He tilled the land and sowed the seed therein, but when the crops grew they stood in need of a strict guard. Nanak, who was always engaged in his meditation, showed himself incapable of turning trespassing cattle out of them. The crops were thus utterly destroyed by the cattle before Kalu could gather them. Kalu was very indignant when he came to know of this, but the *Janamsakhis*, perhaps out of great reverence, which their authors had for Guru Nanak, are silent as to what treatment was then accorded to Nanak by his father.

On his *upnayana sanskara*, i. e., the ceremony of wearing the sacred thread of *yagyopawit*, Nanak asked the *Pundit* why he was to wear the thread that was being administered to him, and on the occasion of whose ceremony the festivities were being held. The *Pundit* told him that it was the sacred thread of yagyopwit or *janeu*, by wearing which he was to enter upon a new life of high morals and noble deeds. It was to make him *dwij*, twice-born. All men of higher castes were enjoined by the *Vedas* to wear the sacred thread. It was strange, said the *Pundit* that a youth born in a Kshatriya family should question about it. "Nay," said Nanak, "it is not then the proper thread that you are administering to me and which is to initiate me into a higher life. Thread symbolises man's binding down his passions. If men and women do not check their passions and indulge in shameless sins every day; if their feet, hands, tongue and eyes are not restrained (from committing sins); of what value is this thread? You go thread-less then, O Brahman! And having spun one from cotton administer it to others. You perform ceremonies on happy occasions, having received wages for the same, and you pretend to show the way to others from your calendars. Hear, O people, this sort of greatness! This man's mind is blind, and still he calls himself a sage![7] This thread is purchased from the *bazar*, and is administered on a purified spot by a Brahman, who whispers some teachings into the ears (of the candidate) and claims to be his *guru* (spiritual leader). But when the man dies, this thread is left behind and his sprit

---

7 Asa di var, M I *shlok* 15 (4)

ਤਗੁ ਨ ਇੰਦ੍ਰੀ, ਤਗੁ ਨ ਨਾਰੀ,
ਭਲਕੇ ਥੁਕ ਪਵੈ ਨਿਤ ਦਾੜੀ,
ਤਗੁ ਨ ਪੈਰੀ, ਤਗੁ ਨ ਹਥੀ,
ਤਗੁ ਨ ਜਿਹਵਾ, ਤਗੁ ਨ ਅਖੀ;
ਵੇਤਗਾ ਆਪੇ ਵਤੈ,
ਵਟਿ ਧਾਗੇ ਅਵਰਾ ਘਤੈ।
ਲੈ ਭਾੜਿ ਕਰੇ ਵੀਆਹੁ,
ਕਢਿ ਕਾਗਲੁ ਦਸੇ ਰਾਹੁ।
ਸੁਣਿ ਵੇਖਹੁ, ਲੋਕਾ, ਇਹੁ ਵਿਡਾਣੁ !
ਮਨਿ ਅੰਧਾ, ਨਾਉ ਸੁਜਾਣੁ॥

goes away threadless. All his theft, debaucheries, falsehoods, abuses, robberies and scandals follow him, night and day. The thread is spun from cotton by a Brahman, and, on a happy day when a he-goat is killed for a feast, all say, 'Wear'. When it is worn out, it is thrown away and a new one is worn. Look, ye people, this thread should not break, if it has any force or efficacy."[8]

This baffled the *pundit* and he enquired if Nanak would not wear it ; to which Nanak replied as follows:-

"Yes, get the thread of contentment from the cotton of compassion, by giving it twists of truth and ties of self-control, and administer it to me, if you can; for this is the *yagyopwit* which the spirit is in need of. This is neither broken, nor gets filthy, is neither burnt, nor gets worn out. Blessed is the man who goes with this on his person."[9]

The above incident, as well as the aforesaid incident at the village school, may appear strange to modern rationalism; but the unquestionable authencity of the *shabads* which were uttered by Guru Nanak, on the two occasions, the practice of

---

8 Asa di *var* M.I. *shlok* 15 (1) and (2)

ਚਉਕੜਿ ਮੁਲਿ ਅਣਾਇਆ, ਬਹਿ ਚਉਕੇ ਪਾਇਆ,
ਸਿਖਾਂ ਕੰਨੀ ਚੜ੍ਹਾਈਆਂ, ਗੁਰ ਬ੍ਰਾਹਮਣ ਥੀਆ,
ਓਹੁ ਮੁਆ, ਓਹੁ ਝੜਿ ਪਇਆ, ਵੇਤਗਾ ਗਇਆ।
ਲਖ ਚੋਰੀਆਂ, ਲਖ ਜਾਰੀਆਂ, ਲਖ ਕੂੜੀਆਂ, ਲਖ ਗਾਲਿ,
ਲਖ ਠਗੀਆਂ, ਪਹਿਨਾਮੀਆਂ, ਰਾਤਿ ਦਿਨ ਸੁ ਜੀਆ ਨਾਲਿ।
ਤਗੁ ਕਪਾਹਹੁ ਕਤੀਐ, ਬਾਹਮਣੁ ਵਟੇ ਆਇ,
ਕੁਹਿ ਬਕਰਾ ਰਿਨੁ ਖਾਇਆ, ਸਭੁ ਕੋ ਆਖੈ 'ਪਾਇ '।
ਹੋਇ ਪੁਰਾਣਾ, ਸੁਟੀਐ, ਭੀ ਫਿਰਿ ਪਾਈਐ ਹੋਰੁ;
ਨਾਨਕ ਤਗੁ ਨ ਤੁਟਈ, ਜੇ ਤਗਿ ਹੋਵੈ ਜੋਰੁ॥
9 Asa di var, M. I *Shlok* 15 (1)
ਦਇਆ ਕਪਾਹ, ਸੰਤੋਖੁ ਸੂਤੁ, ਜਤੁ ਗੰਢੀ, ਸਤੁ ਵਟੁ;
ਏਹੁ ਜਨੇਊ ਜੀਅ ਕਾ, ਹਈ ਤਾ ਪਾਂਡੇ ਘਤੁ।
ਨਾ ਏਹੁ ਤੁਟੇ, ਨਾ ਮਲੁ ਲਗੇ, ਨ ਏਹੁ ਜਲੇ, ਨ ਜਾਇ;
ਧੰਨੁ ਸੁ ਮਾਣਸ, ਨਾਨਕਾ, ਜੋ ਗਲਿ ਚਲੇ ਪਾਇ॥

the Sikhs in not wearing the sacred thread of the Hindus, and the Divine character which is ascribed to Guru Nanak, at least by his followers, afford a sufficient justification for mentioning them here, at some length.

After this, it appears, Nanak was not molested, for some time for it is in his sixteenth year that we find the next and the last attempt of his father to reclaim him. As a student, as a cowherd and as a farmer, Nanak was held to have been a failure. Now Kalu hit upon a different plan. He gave Nanak Rs. 20, and sent him abroad to make some *khara sauda* (good bargain) with that money. He expected, in this way, to inspire in the mind of the boy an interest for trade. Nanak, accompanied by Bala, a *jat* servant, who was entrusted by Kalu with the care of the young would-be trader, left home. They had not gone very far when they came across a party of *sadhus*(*ascetics*). Nanak came to know that the *sadhus* had had no food for the last several days. He forthwith placed his twenty rupees at their feet. The good *sadhus*, however, wanted food, not money. Nanak thereupon sent Bala to buy up as much provisions as the money would fetch, and they all enjoyed a liberal feast. On his return home, he represented it to be the "best of bargains". This exasperated Kalu against his son, and we find in *Janamsakhis* that Kalu, for the first time, gave Nanak a slap on the face. But Rai Bular heard of the incident and sent for the father and son. The former was offered, and he reluctantly received, Rs. 20, and the latter was taken under the Rai's own protection. But, as the Rai was a Mussalman, Nanak was left to live in the same house with his father for some time more, though it was practically settled that he was to be removed from that situation ere long. Father and son were men of the opposite poles, and it was almost impossible to conciliate the two and bring them together. But not many months passed, when an incident occurred which proved for Kalu the last straw that broke the camel's back. On a morning, when Nanak was returning home after bathing at the village tank, he met a mendicant, with whom he sat down for a while and talked on spiritual subjects.

Before leaving him, he offered him the brass jug which he was carrying in his hand and also the golden finger ring which he was wearing. On his arrival at home, Kalu found this out, and was so much provoked that he turned Nanak out of doors. Now, for the first time in his life, Nanak found himself in a precarious situation. He was not certain whether he should go away from home or not; and, if so, where. It was perhaps yet too early for him to begin his preaching work regularly. Disowned by his father and mother, befriended by none, he was still in an unsettled condition when Rai Bular, his noble friend, came to his aid. The Rai sent for both, the father and the son, but now not with the objective of inducing the former to take the latter back into his home, but to ask him to permit Nanak to be sent to his sister, *Bibi* Nanki, who, it may be pointed out, was married, some time before this incident, to *Lala* Jai Ram of Sultanpore. The love that was known to exist between the brother and sister, the recommendation of Rai Bular, and Kalu's own wish to be relieved of the sight of an undutiful son, as he thought Nanak to be, soon helped to the determination of this proposal. Guru Nanak, accompanied by Bala, for the first time left Talwandi, the scene of his early doings, for an indefinite period, in November, 1487. He reached Sultanpore five days after his start, and was affectionately and cheerfully received by his sister and brother-in-law.

This early spiritual bent of mind and indifference to everything earthly may lead some to conjecture that Nanak was an *ascetic*, but it may be pointed out that he never renounced his connection with the world. He had a higher mission than his own salvation. He desired also to save the world along with himself. It seems that, even in these early years, he was conscious of his mission; for notwithstanding his dislike of the ways of the world, and liking, aye, almost affection, for the *faqirs*, he never actually became a follower of them. His early habits were those of reticence, reserve, contemplation and constant solitude. An ordinary man of these habits, under favourable circumstances, and a little inducement, express or tacit, by some mendicant, would easily have become a mendicant himself. But Guru Nanak, though possessed of this powerful inclination, did not renounce the world, *because he did not wish to leave the world behind himself.*

It may here be pointed out that *Maulvi* Ghulam Muhammad, author of the *Siyar-ul-Mutakharin,* who has, in this instance, been quoted by Mr. Muhammad Latif, a Mussalman complier of the "*History of the Punjab*", was probably under the influence of religious enthusiasm and sectarian feeling, when he alleged that *Baba* Nanak was a pupil of Seid Hussain, and had passed his early life in the company of that Moslem devotee. "Nanak was the son of a Grain Merchant," says Ghulam Muhammad, "of the khatri tribe, who, in his youth, was as remarkable for his good character as for the beauty of his person, and for his talents. Nor was he destitute of fortune. There was then, in those parts, a *dervish* of note, called Seid Hussain, a man of eloquence as well as of wealth, who, having no children of his own, and being struck with the beauty of the young Nanak, conceived a great regard for him, and charged himself with his education. As the young man was early introduced to the knowledge of the most esteemed writings of Islam, and initiated into the principles of our (Moslem) most approved doctrines, he advanced so much in learning, and became so fond of his studies, that he made it a practice, in his leisure hours, to translate literally and make notes and extracts of our (Moslem) moral maxims. Those which made the deepest impression upon him were written in the idiom of the Punjab, his maternal language. At length he connected them into order, and put them into verse. By this time, he had so far shaken off those prejudices of Hinduism which had imbibed with his milk, that he became quite another man. His collection became extensive, it took the form of a book, which he entitled *Granth,* and he became famous in the times of Emperor Baber, from which time he was followed by multitudes of converts." The sentiments contained in the above quotation are a sufficient justification for its length, and one single inference which can be gathered out of it is pertinacity with which Guru Nanak was claimed by his Hindu and Muhammadan countrymen alike. And this is quite consistent with the sentiments which were expressed by the two sects at his funeral. But, apart from this, so far as facts are concerned, there is hardly any force in the position taken up by the learned Maulavi. He did not perhaps care to note that nowhere in his life do we find Guru Nanak as a scholar, except on the one occasion, already noted, when he was put by his father to the village school, and where too the period of his scholarship did not extend for more than a few days. Neither is it true that Guru Nanak ever left his village and home to study under any one's instruction elsewhere, nor could his parents entrust him to a Muhammadan devotee to take entire charge of his education, so as to be "early introduced to the knowledge of the most exteemed writings of Islam, and initiated into the principles of our (*Maulvi's*) most approved doctrines."

The position taken up by the *Maulvi* that Guru Nanak "made it a practice in his leisure hours to translate literally and make notes and extracts of the moral maxims of Islam," and wrote them in the idiom of the Punjab, and connecting them into order and putting them into verse, "he entitled" the collection, that became extensive, as the *granth* is equally untenable. No sayings of Guru Nanak, as contained in *Granth Sahib*, have been quoted to us, nor could any be found, to show that they were literally translated or even adapted from any maxims peculiar to Islam. On the contrary, we constantly come across his sayings which go against the popularly accepted doctrines of Islam. Nor is it true that Guru Nanak connected them into order, for his sayings were only preserved from total extinction and oblivion, partly by the efforts of his successor Guru Angad, who put those that he heard or found in scattered scraps into writings, and mostly by the noble work of Guru Arjan Dev, who, *and not Guru Nanak* as the *Maulvi* says, compiled and entitled the *Granth*.

To show the utter absurdity of the *Maulvi's* assertion it may further be observed that Seid Hussain had not most probably yet begUn his life when Guru Nanak was already in the height of his glory. One Seid Hussain, we know, was a contemporary of the fifth Guru, by whom were rejected the Seid's sayings as unworthy of being included in the *Granth*, because they were *not consistent* Sikh doctrines. Another Seid Hussain of any importance has not yet been found to have ever existed.

Another note as to the teachership of Guru Nanak has somewhere been struck, which seems to have been generally resounded by most of the European writers on Guru Nanak, though without quoting their source, that Guru Nanak was a pupil of Bhagat Kabir of Benares. It seems true that Guru Nanak did meet Bhagat Kabir at Benares during his travels, and the two reformers did interchange ideas for some time. But there is hardly any authority for ascribing to Bhagat Kabir the teachership of Guru Nanak. As has been shown above, Guru Nanak never left his native village up to the end of his nineteenth year, and then too he left it only for Sultanpore, where *alone* he remained for the next thirteen years or so. His biographies do not show that he visited any third place, excepting, of course, the native village of his wife, during this long period, and it is also not shown where he received his lessons from Bhagat Kabir.

಄಄

CHAPTER 3
BUSINESS

The short sketch of Guru Nanak's early life which has been given in the last chapter must have shown to the reader that Guru Nanak was one of those who are occasionally sent by God into this world on a special deputation to reform and save her. He was still young when he commenced his work and began first at home.

Some superficial readers have attempted to cast a slur on the illustrious name of Nanak, and have vaguely asserted that he took the religious life as he was an utter failure in his secular dealings. This they seem to gather from the over-anxiety of *Mehta* Kalu, on account of his son's failure in business. It is also true that Guru Nanak who was naturally of a religious bent of mind, and who was not in fact created to materially prosper in the world, did show in his early life that he was not made to succeed in the world, in the sense his father wished him to do. But these men, in bringing this charge against Guru Nanak, seem to have utterly lost sight of about 12 years of his life that he spent as *Modi* to the Nawab Daulat Khan Lodhi of Sultanpore. It was shortly[10] after his arrival at his sister's place that his brother-in-law, Jai Ram, secured, at his request, for

---

10 Only 8 days after his arrival it is said, he entered upon his duties in *modikhana*.

him, the post of *Modi,* whose duties were to supply necessaries for the Nawab's household and retainers, at the contract rates, which post was then lying vacant. That he quite succeeded in this business will be apparent from what is to follow.

Mr. Muhammad Latif in his *History of the Punjab* says that Nanak was put in charge of the charity house of the Nawab. But it is also to be observed that a *modikhana* is not at all a charity house, nor were the Lodhis ever famous for their charity. The duties of a *modi* were almost what those of a commissariat Agent and Storekeeper are today. Money was, from time to time, advanced by Government to the *Modi* to purchase and supply, when needed, provisions to the Nawab. At the *modikhana,* Guru Nanak used to extend his helping hand to the poor, so much so that after supplying his own family wants, he would give away a large part of his earnings in charity to the needy. This led several times to a *bazar* rumour to the effect that Nanak was running into bankruptcy and was squandering the Government money. These rumours reaching the Nawab, the accounts were checked. If Mr. Muhammad Latif's assertion were true, it would be hard, in the first place, for a man to keep exact accounts of a charity house, so as to put them before the competent men to check them; and, in the next place, the Nawab would not have taken action on mere *bazar* rumour that Nanak was freely distributing Government stores and money in charity to the *faqirs* because that would have been the very performance of his duties. We know for certain that several times and, among them, twice on account of the said *bazar* rumours, these accounts were checked; and we also know that the result of the special checking on the two occasions was that the Government of Nawab was found to owe several hundreds of rupees to Nanak, as the supplies actually taken out had exceeded the money advanced to him till then. Here too, Mr. Muhammad Latif's theory fails; for, had it been a charity house, the Nawab could not have been found owing anything to Nanak.

When Nanak took over the charge of the *modikhana*, Bala, who was still staying with him, asked his permission to return home; but Nanak told him to stay on and work with him at the *modikhana*. Nanak told him, in words which could not be mistaken, that the business which he had then entered upon was not *his*; that it was simply a means to pass the days; and that *his real work* was still lying undone before him. Of his *real business* he had given a faint indication in the "True Bargain" already mentioned. Thus Bala remained with him throughout the period which he spent in the *modikhana*.

Shortly after his appointment, Guru Nanak married, in June 1488, *Bibi* Sulakhani, daughter of *Lala* Mul Chand of Pakhoke, in the Gurdaspur district.

During this period, too, it seems that he did not lose sight of his mission, even for a moment. At the time of his marriage, he was asked by Mardana[11] for some gift (*bakhshish*), but, instead of giving him any pecuniary gift, Nanak gifted him with the divine art of music. Ever afterwards, Mardana was reputed to be one of the best musicians. He also told Mardana, in the course of his talk, that his real work was a different one, which he had not lost sight of, and that his present employment was only for the purpose of completing his days.

Guru Nanak had two sons out of his marriage with Sulakhni. The first, who was born in July, 1494, was named Sri Chand, and the second, born in February, 1497, was named Lakhmi Chand. On the thirteenth day after the birth of Sri Chand, when Guru Nanak returned home from his *modikhana,* for his breakfast, he found that preparations were being made for the ceremony of purifying the house, from the *sutak,* which had attached to all articles in the house on account of the birth in it of a child.

---

11 Mardana was by caste a Mirasi, a low caste whose members only play upon the harp and beat drum on happy occasions. In the Punjab these Mirasi know very little of music and generally employed by Hindu and Muhammadan population menial services of various kind. Each Mirasi is attached to a group of families in his village who are called his jajmans (Clients) because they support him and his family in return for his services.

In consequence of this supposed pollution, which attaches not only to everything in the house but also to every human being belonging to that family and even to that caste, no Brahman is allowed to partake of food or water from that house, or from the hands of the members of that family and caste. About these preparations Guru Nanak seems to have been quite ignorant, untill his coming home; and, from what was already known of Nanak, it is also quite natural and probable that he was not consulted beforehand. For when he came home and saw the *Pundit* with his usual appliances, he enquired what was all that fuss about. The *Pundit* told him that, according to the *Shastras*, everything in the house became polluted by a birth of death therein, and they could only be purified by performing the ceremony which the *Shastras* had laid down for it. But hardly did the *Pundit* conceive that, in laying down this proposition, he was practically admitting that the house could never be pure. "If we do believe in the *sutak*," said Nanak, "then there will ever and always be *sutak*." So many living creatures are in the cowdung[12] and other fuel (produced and burnt); no grain of corn is without a living being; nay, the very water which satiates all, contains living beings. How, then, can this impurity be kept off, when it is always present in our kitchens and food. The *sutak* then cannot be washed away but by the knowledge of GOD."[13] (by which alone these absurd notions can be got rid of) "All *sutak*," he continued, "is a matter of superstition, for it recognises other than the truth. Birth and death are the order of God, by Whose Will is the coming and going (to and from

---

12 People in Punjab generally burn dried cakes of cowdung as fuel.
13 Asa di *var* M. 1, *Shlok* 18(1)

ਜੇਕਰਿ ਸੁਤਕੁ ਮਨੀਐ, ਸਭ ਤੈ ਸੁਤਕੁ ਹੋਇ।
ਗੋਹੇ ਅਤੈ ਲਕੜੀ ਅੰਦਰਿ ਕੀੜਾ ਹੋਇ;
ਜੇਤੇ ਦਾਣੇ ਅੰਨ ਕੇ ਜੀਆ ਬਾਝੁ ਨ ਕੋਇ;
ਪਹਿਲਾ ਪਾਣੀ ਜੀਉ ਹੈ, ਜਿਤੁ ਹਰਿਆ ਸਭੁ ਕੋਇ;
ਸੁਤਕੁ ਕਿਉ ਕਰ ਰਖੀਐ, ਸੁਤਕੁ ਪਵੈ ਰਸੋਈ;
ਨਾਨਕ, ਸੁਤਕੁ ਏਵ ਨ ਉਤਰੈ; ਗਿਆਨੁ ਉਤਾਰੇ ਧੋਇ।।

this world). All drinking and eating is pure, for all food is sent by Him. No *sutak* sticks to those who have comprehended the Truth."14 The *pundit* was thus taken unawares and got puzzled in his mind. But he mustered courage to ask Nanak if all the *Vedas* and *Shastras* were mistaken in laying down this ceremony, and if, in his opinion, there was no *sutak*. Nanak's reply to this question was in the affirmative. "Covetousness," he said, "was the *sutak* of the mind and lie of the tongue; looking at another's wife, beauty and riches, is that of the eyes, and of the ears is the hearing of false tales. With these impurities man goeth tied up to the city of Yama (hell)."15 This ended the disputation and the *pundit* was gently asked to leave at once.

One day, Guru Nanak was weighing out provisions to the steward of the Nawab. The weight in his scale-pan was a five-seers one, and he had to count the number of times he was weighing out the article. When in so counting, he reached the number thirteen (*tera*, which in Punjabi also means 'thine'), his mind at once travelled beyond the earthly thing that he was weighing, and transplanted itself on the Almighty Father, calling *tera, tera* (Thine, Thine); while mechanically he went on weighing the article. His mind, transfixed on the Divine, would not stoop to the earthly things, and all subsequent *dharans* went for the *thirteenth*. At this juncture, the attention of Bala, the servant was attracted who at once advanced and caught his arm to stop him from

---

14 Asa di var, M. 1, *shlok* 18(3)
ਸਭੇ ਸੂਤਕੁ ਭਰਮੁ ਹੈ, ਦੂਜੈ ਲਗੈ ਜਾਇ।
ਜਮਣੁ ਮਰਣਾ ਹੁਕਮੁ ਹੈ, ਭਾਣੈ ਆਵੈ ਜਾਇ।
ਖਾਣਾ ਪੀਣਾ ਪਵਿਤੁ ਹੈ, ਦਿਤੋਨੁ ਰਿਜਕੁ ਸੰਬਾਹਿ।
ਨਾਨਕ ਜਿਨੀ ਗੁਰਮੁਖਿ ਬੁਝਿਆ, ਤਿਨਾ ਸੂਤਕੁ ਨਾਹਿ॥
15 Asa din *var* M. 1, *Shlok* 18(2)
ਮਨ ਕਾ ਸੂਤਕੁ ਲੋਭੁ ਹੈ; ਜਿਹਵਾ ਸੂਤਕੁ ਕੂੜੁ;
ਅਖੀ ਸੂਤਕੁ ਵੇਖਣਾ, ਪਰ ਤ੍ਰਿਅ, ਪਰ ਧਨ, ਰੂਪੁ;
ਕੰਨੀ ਸੂਤਕੁ ਕੰਨਿ ਪੈ, ਲਾਇ ਤਬਾਰੀ ਖਾਹਿ;
ਨਾਨਕ ਹੰਸਾ ਆਦਮੀ, ਬਧੇ ਜਮ ਪੁਰਿ ਜਾਹਿ॥

weighing. The article was re-weighted, and, strange to say, it was only 65 seers and no more.

At his home, he performed all the duties incidental to a married life. He looked after the expenses of his wife and family, and saw that all the necessaries were supplied to them properly. No doubt, he did not lay by anything and did not horde any money; and on this account, his wife sometimes complained. Otherwise, as regards her necessaries and comforts, she had no cause to murmur. Whatever he could spare from his family expenses, which were of course very moderate, he spent in meeting the wants of others.

For about 12 years, Guru Nanak led a virtuous married life. By doing business he showed to the world that if he has subsequently left the worldly transactions, it was not on account of his failure therein. He was capable of doing a business and succeeding in life, as much as any virtuous man could be accredited with success. But his mission was a higher and nobler one. He could live in the world, earn a living and support a family, as he had done; but having subdued and killed his earthly passions, he was to save mankind from their dreadful traps. What is the world but the various things, which hinder man's development and advancements towards ideal perfection? Many reformers have been frightened by the world, and hence have become timid and cowardly cold and indifferent to reform. Mathew Arnold wrote the following beautiful sonnet on the "Triumphs of the World" over reformers, who have, from time to time, tried "to recast her new":-

So far as I conceive the world's rebuke
To him address'd who would recast her new,
Now from herself her fame of strength she took,
But from their weakness who would work her rue.

'Behold,' she cries, 'so many rages lull'd,
'So many fiery spirits quite cool'd down;

'Look how so many valours, long undull'd,
'After short commerce with me fear my frown!

'Then too when thou against my crimes wouldst cry
'Let thy foreboded homage check thy tongue!'
The world speaks well; yet might her foe reply:
'Are wills so weak? then let not mine wait long!

'Hast thou so rare a poison? – let me be
'Keener to stay thee, lest thou poison me.'

But Guru Nanak showed to the world that he was above the type of reformers who fear her frown "after short commerce" with her. He proved, in the course of about 12 years, that he was not afraid of world's rebuke; that he was never to render homage to her; that *his will* was not weak; and that he was strong enough to meet her face to face, and yet be, out of her snares. Born with, and for, his mission, to save others from the world's dreadful jaws, to him that "rare poison" was quite harmless; for like the lotus leaf, he had not fixed his mind in the water of the world. He was quite free from, though in close proximity to, her. Living in, and for, the world, he was to raise the latter to his own level.

ᘓ৪ᘒ

CHAPTER 4
RESIGNATION

No *Janamsakhi* gives the details of Guru Nanak's daily life at Sultanpore, but this much can be gathered out of the heap of material presented by these vernacular biographies, that Guru Nanak got up from his bed every morning long before dawn, washed at the stream, and remained absorbed in his contemplation and religious services, till late in the morning. What those services were is not fully known. Then he went to his *modikhana,* remained there for the whole day, except at noon, when he would come home for break-fast. Even in his *modikhana,* it appears, he used to confer on spiritual subjects with the *sadhus,* who used to visit him there; and he also used, now and then, to teach whose who approached him. The evening, up to late in the night, passed in singing hymns in praise of God and in conferring on topics pertaining to the same. To this programme might also be added his occasional visit to his sister, *Bibi* Nanki.

After bathing in the *V'een,* one morning, Guru Nanak plunged into the jungle close by. He became lost for three days. Nobody knew where he was. There was a good deal of talk in *bazar.* Many theories were invented and a good many charges were laid against him. The most common of the charges was that of embezzlement and bankruptcy. The news reached the Nawab and full investigation was ordered to be made into the case. But when his accounts were checked, the State was found to owe a few hundred rupees to Nanak. Thus all those theories crumbled to dust. On the other hand, it can hardly be known where Guru Nanak had gone. His biographer says that he remained for the three days in full communion with God. It is here that his journey to, and attendance at, the Court of the Almighty Father is described, and it is pointed out that God Himself instructed him on this occasion regarding the nature and method of his Mission on Earth. He was given, says the legend, a globet of Water of Life, which he drank, and the voice of the Lord commanded him thus: "Nanak, I am with thee. I have made thee happy; and whoever shall follow thee, I shall make them all happy. Go thou, preach My Name and do not forget Me. Remain uncontaminated from the world. I have given to thee My own Name, do thou this work." In the absence of any other explanation, it is, at any rate, clear and certain that the whole plan of his future work was definitely settled within these three days. For, when he appeared after that interval, or, as the legend goes, when he recovered from his trance, he made his notions and ideas unmistakably clear to those who approached him. He uttered the keynote of his future system in the remarkable phrase, "There is no Hindu; there is no Mussalman." The utterance of such a paradox soon raised a commotion against him, and led many to conjecture that he had turned insane; was possessed of some evil spirit; and so on. The news of his reappearance having reached the Nawab, even he lent ear to such theories, and was anxious to get Nanak cured of his supposed disease or evil spirit. Physicians and *Mullah*s were deputed for his treatment. The incident that followed this is so interesting and instructive that it deserves treatment in full.

At the earnest request of the Nawab (who was also present) to cure Nanak, the *Mullah* first began to dispossess him of the supposed evil spirit, and for that purpose he wrote some words on a piece of paper to tie the amulet round Nanak's neck. When he was writing it, Nanak said:

"No room to gather fruits for him whose crop decay'd.
"Accursed life of him who sells the Name of God.".[16]

But, notwithstanding this, the *Mullah*, anxious, as he was, not to lose the golden opportunity of getting a handsome reward from the Nawab, performed the whole of his ceremony, and enquired, as is usual with men of his class as to which spirit was there, by saying, "Who art thou?"[17] The following was the reply that came out:-

"Some call me *Bhut*, Some call me *Baital*,
"Some human being Nanak call."[18]

On this, it was alleged that no spirit had possessed him, but that he was mad; to which Nanak replied, in the same strain, as follows:-

"Aye, mad is Nanak after Lord!
        "He recognizes none but Him.
"He mad alone, who fears God,
        "And recognises none but Him.
"He mad alone who minds the One,
        "Submits to God, nor trusteth skill.
"He mad alone, who loves the One.

---

16 *Var* Sarang M 1, *Shlok* 20 (1)
ਖੇਤੀ ਜਿਨ ਕੀ ਉਜੜੈ ਖਲਵਾੜੇ ਕਿਆ ਥਾਉ।
ਧ੍ਰਿਗੁ ਤਿਨਾਂ ਕਾ ਜੀਵਿਆ, ਜਿ ਲਿਖਿ ਲਿਖਿ ਵੇਚਹਿ ਨਾਉ।।

17 The prevailing impression with superstitions people is that as long as man is so possessed, it is the spirit that acts and speaks in him and not he himself. Therefore the question is put in this form as being addressed directly to the spirit. It is believed that if there is in reality any evil spirit, it is bound to disclose herself to the expert who puts her such questions.

18 Rag Maru, M. 1, *Shlok* 7(1)
ਕੋਈ ਆਖੈ ਭੂਤਨਾ, ਕੋ ਕਹੈ ਬੇਤਾਲਾ,
ਕੋਈ ਆਖੈ ਆਦਮੀ ਨਾਨਕ ਵੇਚਾਰਾ।

"Himself thinks low, all others high."[19]

After this, the physician stepped forward and began to feel his pulse. At this time, Guru Nanak's heart was beating high, and the physician began to prescribe a medicine for him. But, before he could do so, Guru Nanak addressed him as follows:-

"*Byd* is called to cure, he feels the pulse;
Simple *Byd*, doth know not 'pain in heart.'
Go away, *Byd* do take from me no curse;
Whom doth cure thou? Am in love of God.
Able *Byd*, if diagnose pain,
Findeth cure from woes all to relieve.
Byd comes and finds the cure for man who ails,
"No cure need I,"soul and stuff cries raise.
Go thy way, *Byd,* my disease know Saints.
Easeth from disease Creator, Cause of pains."[20]

---

19 Rag Maru M 1 *Shlok* 7 (2) (3) (4)

ਭਇਆ ਦਿਵਾਨਾ ਸਾਹੁ ਕਾ ਨਾਨਕ ਬਉਰਾਨਾ;
ਹਉ ਹਰਿ ਬੀਨ ਅਵਰੁ ਨ ਜਾਨਾ।
ਤਉ ਦਿਵਾਨਾ ਜਾਣੀਐ ਜਾਂ ਭੈ ਦੇਵਾਨਾ ਹੋਇ,
ਏਕੀ ਸਾਹਿਬ ਬਾਹਰਾ ਦੂਜਾ ਅਵਰੁ ਨ ਜਾਨੈ ਕੋਈ।
ਤਉ ਦੇਵਾਨਾ ਜਾਣੀਐ ਜਾਂ ਏਕਾ ਕਾਰ ਕਮਾਇ,
ਹੁਕਮੁ ਪਛਾਣੈ ਖਸਮ ਕਾ, ਦੂਜੀ ਅਵਰ ਸਿਆਣਪ ਕਾਇ।
ਤਉ ਦੇਵਾਨਾ ਜਾਣੀਐ ਜਉ ਸਾਹਿਬੁ ਧਰੈ ਪਿਆਰੁ,
ਮੰਦਾ ਜਾਣੈ ਆਪ ਕਉ, ਅਵਰੁ ਭਲਾ ਸੰਸਾਰੁ।।

20 Vide *Bhai Ditt singh's Janamsakhi* of Guru Nanak. Also *Bhai* Bala's *Janamsakhi*. In the both them this story of physician is stated as having occurred long before this occasion. The first two lines also occure in *Var Malar*, M. 1, *Shlok* 3(1)

ਵੈਦੁ ਬੁਲਾਇਆ ਵੈਦਗੀ, ਪਕੜਿ ਢੰਢੋਲੇ ਬਾਂਹ;
ਭੋਲਾ ਵੈਦ ਨ ਜਾਣਈ ਕਰਕ ਕਲੇਜੇ ਮਾਹਿ।।
ਜਾਹਿ ਵੈਦ ਘਰ ਆਪਣੈ, ਮੇਰੀ ਆਹਿ ਨ ਲੇਹੁ;
ਹਮ ਰਤੇ ਸਹੁ ਆਪਣੈ, ਤੂ ਕਿਸ ਦਾਰੂ ਦੇਹੁ ?
ਬੈਦਾ ਬੈਦ ਸੁਜਾਨ ਤੂ ਪਹਲਾ ਰੋਗ ਪਛਾਣ;

On hearing this, the *Mullah*, the Kazi, the physician and others declared that Guru Nanak was neither possessed, nor mad, nor diseased; but that his heart was full of devotion to, and love of, God, and he was, therefore, indifferent to earthly things. Now the Nawab held a council with the *Mullah* and the Kazi, and then proposed to Guru Nanak that, if he was really devoted to one God, then he might accompany them to the Musjid, to pray to the Lord in their company; for they also recognised that "there is no God but God." This Nanak readily consented to do. The party came to the Musjid and began to pray, according to the Muhammadan style; but, strange to say, Nanak did not join them while praying. When they had finished, the Nawab asked Nanak why he had not joined them, as promised. On this, Guru Nanak questioned as to who was praying to God that he could have joined. "I," said Nawab; to which Guru Nanak replied:-

"Thou strukst thy forehead on the earth,
"Thy mind did travel in the sky,
"Well listen, Daulat Khan Afghan
"To Kabul horses went to buy."[21]

On hearing this, the Nawab was abashed, but he said, "Well, you could then have joined others, and, among them, the noble Kazi;" To which Guru Nanak's reply was that the mind of Kazi was, at the time of the prayer, following his colt, lest it may fall down into the pit in his courtyard. Both the Nawab and

ਐਸਾ ਦਾਰੂ ਲੋੜ ਲਹੁ ਜਿਸ ਵੰਵੇ ਰੋਗਾਂ ਘਾਣ।
ਦੁਖ ਲਗੇ ਦਾਰੂ ਘਣਾ ਬੈਦ ਖਲੋਇਆ ਆਇ;
ਕਾਇਆ ਰੋਵੇ, ਹੰਸ ਪੁਕਾਰੇ, ਵੈਦ ਨ ਦਾਰੂ ਲਾਇ।
ਜਾਇ ਬੈਦ ਘਰ ਆਪਣੇ, ਜਾਣੇ ਕੋਈ ਮਕੋਈ।
ਜਿਨ ਕਰਤੇ ਦੁਖ ਲਾਇਆ, ਨਾਨਕ ਲਾਹੇ ਸੋਇ।।
21 *Bhai* Bala's *Janamsakhi*
ਮੱਥਾ ਠੋਕੇ ਜ਼ਿਮੀ ਪਰ, ਦਿਲ ਉਠੇ ਅਸਮਾਨ,
ਘੋੜੇ ਕਾਬਲ ਖਰੀਦ ਕਰੇ ਦੌਲਤ ਖ਼ਾਨ ਪਠਾਨ।।

the Kazi were silenced, because they felt the point of the true remarks. Thereupon, followed the sermon of Guru Nanak on Islam, as to what it really was and what they had taken it to be. This was his first regular sermon after his resignation of the world. It was at once destructive as well as constructive in its nature. The vain glories of the Muhammadans were all exposed therein, and the Nawab, the Kazi, the *Mullah* and others, listened spellbound to the words of truth, which fearlessly left the Guru's lips.

"It is difficult," said Nanak, "to be a real Mussalman." First, have the necessary qualities, and then call yourselves Moslem. First of all, Love your faith, and leave off vain glory and pride of riches. Be humble and sure of salvation. Submit to God with patience, believe in Him and lose yourselves in Him. Be kind to all living beings, then alone you can call yourselves Mussalman.[22] Compassion should be your Musjid; sincerity your prayer-carpet; and honesty your *Al Qoran*. Let modesty be your circumcision, and amiability your fasting, which befit a Mussalman. Let good deeds be your *Kaaba*, truth your *Kalma* and charity your prayer. Acquire meekness for your rosary, and thus be honoured before God.[23] Others, dues are like pork to one and like beef to others, and remember that the prophet too will claim you only if you will not eat what is so forbidden. Mere

---

22 *Var* Majh, M, 1 *Shlok* 8(1)

ਮੁਸਲਮਾਣੁ ਕਹਾਵਣੁ ਮੁਸਕਲੁ ਜਾਂ ਹੋਈ ਤਾਂ ਮੁਸਲਮਾਣੁ ਕਹਾਵੈ।
ਅਵਲਿ ਅਉਲਿ ਦੀਨੁ ਕਰਿ ਮਿਠਾ, ਮੁਸਕਲ ਮਾਨਾ ਮਾਲੁ ਮੁਸਾਵੈ।
ਹੋਇ ਮੁਸਲਿਮੁ ਦੀਨ ਮੁਹਾਣੈ ਮਰਣ ਜੀਵਣ ਕਾ ਭਰਮੁ ਚੁਕਾਵੈ।
ਰਬ ਕੀ ਰਜਾਇ ਮੰਨੇ ਸਿਰ ਉਪਰਿ ਕਰਤਾ ਮੰਨੇ ਆਪੁ ਗਵਾਵੈ।
ਤਉ ਨਾਨਕ ਸਰਬ ਜੀਆ ਮਿਹਰੰਮਤਿ ਹੋਇ ਤ ਮੁਸਲਮਾਣੁ ਕਹਾਵੈ॥
23 *Var* Majh, M. 1 *Shlok* 7(1)

ਮਿਹਰ ਮਸੀਤਿ, ਸਿਦਕੁ ਮੁਸੱਲਾ, ਹਕੁ ਹਲਾਲੁਕੁਰਾਣੁ।
ਸ਼ਰਮ ਸੁੰਨੀਤ, ਸੀਲੁ ਰੋਜਾ, ਹੋਹੁ ਮੁਸਲਮਾਣੁ।
ਕਰਣੀ ਕਾਬਾ, ਸਚੁ ਪੀਰੁ ਕਲਮਾ, ਕਰਮ ਨਿਵਾਜਾ।
ਤਸਬੀ ਸ਼ਾਂਤਿ ਸੁਭਾਵਸੀ, ਨਾਨਕ ਰਖੈ ਲਾਜ॥

talk cannot take you to paradise. Truth and sincerity alone will lead to your emancipation. Whatever is unlawful for you does not become lawful by being seasoned. So too, by these false ways of yours, you will have but false things; (in other words, truth will not be acquired by falsity, although seasoned with appearances).[24] There are five prayers for five different times and with as many different names. Let "truth" be your first prayer; "lawful acquisitions," the second; "charity," the third; "sincerity of mind," the fourth; and "to praise God's qualities," the fifth. Let good actions be your *Kalma;* and then alone will you be Mussalman. Otherwise, remember that, on account of the falsity of ways, only false things are acquired by people who deal in false things."[25]

So saying, Guru Nanak left the Musjid and was followed by a large number of people. But the Nawab wanted to ask his wish with regard to the money that was due to him from the State. Guru Nanak, however, refused to receive it himself and advised the Nawab to spend it in meeting the wants of the poor.[26]

---

24 Var Majh, M. I *Shlok* 7(2)

ਹਕੁ ਪਰਾਇਆ ਨਾਨਕਾ, ਉਸੁ ਸੂਅਰ, ਉਸੁ ਗਾਇ।
ਗੁਰ ਪੀਰੁ ਹਾਮਾ ਤਾਂ ਭਰੇ, ਜ ਮੁਰਦਾਰੁ ਨ ਖਾਇ।
ਗਲੀ ਭਿਸ਼ਤਿ ਨ ਜਾਈਐ, ਛੁਟੈ ਸਚੁ ਕਮਾਇ।
ਮਾਰਣ ਪਾਹਿ ਹਰਾਮ ਮਹਿ, ਹੋਇ ਹਲਾਲੁ ਨ ਜਾਇ।
ਨਾਨਕ ਗਲੀ ਕੁੜੀ ਟੀ, ਕੁੜੇ ਪਲੈ ਪਾਇ।।

25 Var Majh, M. 1, *Shlok* 7(3)

ਪੰਜਿ ਨਿਵਾਜਾਂ, ਵਖਤ ਪੰਜਿ, ਪੰਜਾਂ ਪੰਜੇ ਨਾਉਂ।
ਪਹਿਲਾ ਸਚੁ, ਹਲਾਲ ਦੁਇ, ਤੀਜਾ ਖੈਰ ਖੁਦਾਇ,
ਚਉਥੀ ਨੀਅਤਿ ਰਾਸਿ ਮਨੁ, ਪੰਜਵੀ ਸਿਫਤਿ ਸਨਾਇ।
ਕਰਣੀ ਕਲਮਾ ਆਖਿਕੈ, ਮੁਸਲਮਾਣੁ ਸਦਾਇ।
ਨਾਨਕ ਜੇਤੇ ਕੁੜਿਆਰ, ਕੁੜੇ ਕੁੜੀ ਪਾਇ।।

26 It is stated that, later on, *Lala* Mul Chand, father-in-law of Guru Nank, arrived, and obtaining an audience of the Nawab, he appealed in favour of his daughter. Now Guru Nanak could not be found, and, therefore, a compromise was entered into, according to which Nawab paid half of the amount to Mul Chand for Guru Nanak's wife and sons, and the other half was spent according to Guru Nanak's Gift.

After this, Guru Nanak paid a visit to his sister, *Bibi* Nanki, and to his wife and children and then again left the town. It was with difficulty that he could prevail upon his wife to remain at home, while he *had* to go abroad. His wife was strongly opposed to his leaving home. But his sister, *Bibi* Nanki, did not press him much, for she fully understood her brother, from his very childhood, and was proud of him. The fact that *Bibi* Nanki was the only one of Guru Nanak's relatives, who instead of opposing him in his mission, encouraged him and even assisted him, in her own way, is remarkable and testifies to her devotion to her brother's cause, and love for his person. She requested Guru Nanak to visit her, now and then, so that she may not feel the absence of the ennobling soul for any considerable time, and may not forget any of his holy and noble ideas. This request of one so deeply attached was most affectionately accepted and was never forgotten.

ॐ

CHAPTER 5
FIRST DISCIPLE
AND COMPANION

The news of the Guru's resignation and of what followed it, spread rapidly and reached Talwandi in no time. *Mehta* Kalu sent Mardana to Sultanpore to verify the rumour and to induce Nanak, if need to, abandon his idea of *faqiri*. Mardana was instructed to strain every nerve to bring Nanak back to his home. He was to be reminded of all his connections. The condition of his wife and children after him was to be drawn before his eyes and his *heart* was to be appealed to, as it was the heart that played the foremost part in him. With this mission Mardana reached Sultanpore, when Guru Nanak had already left the town again and was residing in jungle. Mardana followed him there and received a cordial welcome, as if Guru Nanak was already waiting for him. Such was the force of Guru Nanak's personality that Mardana could not even open his lips to fulfil his mission, and, instead of converting the Guru, for which object he had come, he himself became a convert and disciple. He determined to spend the rest of his life in the Guru's service, notwithstanding the Guru telling him that he would have to suffer hunger and privations, in so doing. Guru Nanak, who was an apostle of the doctrine of brother-hood of man as man, readily conferred on him the title of "*Bhai*," brother, irrespective of his low origin and caste. It was the inherent virtue and devotion to God, and not the birth, caste, riches, title, lands, estates, nor worldly offices, which gave superiority to man in the Kingdom of Heaven. *Bhakti* alone could lead to man's emancipation, and unflinching Faith was the necessary requisite for the attainment of eternal bliss. And Mardana, in whose person the Guru's power was already working in the shape of music, was not found wanting in faith and devotion on this occasion, and, being supplied with a rebeck, had the honor of remaining throughout his life, a companion of the Guru. He was the first disciple of Guru Nanak.

Bala's name is also generally associated with that of Mardana, as being Guru Nanak's life-companion, but it seems that the fact cannot be established in its totality. Bala seems to have left Guru Nanak for home, when the latter resigned the *modikhana*. The *Janamsakhi*s agree that although rumour had already reached Talwandi about Guru Nanak's resignation, the details were carried there by Bala. The mention in the *Janamsakhi*s, which generally go under the name of Bala as their author, though existing in various different and inconsistent versions, of Bala as Guru Nanak's *life-companion,* seems to have been the work of Bala's descendants, who, when Guru Nanak's mission became universally popular long after him, seem not to have liked to remain behind to claim that *their* ancestor was also an indispensable helpmate of the Guru. And, for this purpose, they seem to have made a good many interpolations in the *Janamsakhi*s. Otherwise, the oldest extant *Janamsakhi*, the manuscript of which is lying in the India Office, London although the prefect authencity of that even cannot be vouchsafed, does not make mention of him. It may, moreover, be observed that, although in these later *Janamsakhi*s mention is made of Bala's name, yet nowhere do we find him taking any part in the conversation or talk with the Guru or other Sikhs or serving him in any way; *except* on the two occasions, noticed before, when the subject of his service was simply of a business nature; while Mardana makes frequent appearance on the stage. Thus it seems tolerably certain that Bala, who was appointed to serve Guru Nanak twice in business matters, left the company of his master when the business ended. Whether he did so voluntarily or as bidden by Guru Nanak himself, we cannot say for certain. But it seems that he could not have done so of his own accord. Having spent such a long period in the Guru's service at the *modikhana*, it cannot be held for a moment that he was not raised to a high level of purity of life and *Bhakti*, and if this was so, he would have naturally desired to remain with his master wherever the latter went. But he would have been an unnecessary adjunct to the Guru, for, if Mardana was allowed and even asked to accompany Guru Nanak, it was on account of his music attainments. Therefore, it seems that Guru Nanak did not like Bala to leave home and make an unnecessary retinue for him, and so advised him to stay with his own family at Talwandi. It is possibly true that when, after the death of Mardana, Guru Nanak visited Talwandi to take another companion from there, he took Bala as well as Sajada, a son of Mardana, with himself; but Sajada's early separation left him again one companion only is the person of Bala. This last companionship of Bala, if admitted, seems to have continued till the end of Guru Nanak's life.

In the pictures of Guru Nanak, which are popular, it will be noticed that, Bala is shown as holding *chaur* over Guru Nanak's head, thus indicating that Bala always occupied a place close to the Guru. But if the suggestion, mentioned above, about interpolations in the *Janamsakhi*s be accepted, the explanation for the arrangement of the group does not seem to be very difficult. The most remarkable thing to be noticed in the said group, however, is that, whereas both Guru Nanak and Mardana, in the said portrait are shown to have got white hair, Bala appears with a black beard. From this it may very well be inferred that the group was prepared long after Guru Nanak, that all the three individuals had probably separate pictures before, that bala had his hair black when *his* picture was drawn, and that *that* was probably the time when he was a companion of Guru Nanak. This would support the view enunciated above that Bala, after leaving Guru Nanak's company, on the latter's resigning the *modikhana,* did not accompany him in his travels.

ॐ

CHAPTER 6
TRAVELS

It is almost impossible to write a true and connected account of Guru Nanak's Travels at this distance of time. The *Janamsakhis* give such a disconnected, confused and mixed up description of them that a good deal of it seems to be fictitious and misleading. It is really a matter of deep regret that we should have no authentic record of the travels of such a good Reformer, who worked only four hundred years ago and who spread the Gospel of Love and Righteousness, not only in the whole of India but also carried it to Turkey and Arabia in the West, Siam and Burma in the East, Ceylon in the South and Kashmere in the North - in short, through-out the whole of Sothern Asia. Whatever is preserved to us of his history are a number of fragments of historical incidents, disconnected with each other, forming more a book of anecdotes form his life than a biography of his. His chronicle has reached us only in scattered narratives lacking in chronological exactness. But in these scattered incidents, mixed up with fictitious tales, may be discerned the development of the same powerful character, the growth of the same living personality, and everywhere is clearly visible the powerful presence of the same living breath, the same sincere and earnest heart, which first manifested itself in his early life at home, and then in the Musjid at Sultanpore.

His sayings, so well and authentically preserved to us by the noble efforts of Guru Arjan Dev, the fifth Guru, shall ever act as touchstone for us, when we are engaged in studying his Life and Character. In all that has gone before and all that is to follow, in this narrative, the incidents have been recorded, as verified by the Guru's sayings, or regarding which all the *Janamsakhi*s have agreed, or as to the authencity of which no doubt could be entertained. In this chapter, the route of Guru Nanak's travels will be traced, so far as it is possible, and some of the incidents will be narrated in regular order. Others will be dealt with in the next chapter without any reference to their chronology. The travels seem to have begun though the date is not quite certain in 1500, of the Christian era.

When Guru Nanak started on his tour, he seems first to have visited Amenabad in the Gujranwala district, where he went straight to the house of one, Lalo, a carpenter. Lalo was preparing wooden pegs when the voice aroused him, "Lalo, what art thou doing?" Such was the influence of Guru Nanak's personality that Lalo looked above and at once threw himself down on the visitor's feet. What followed this introduction is more or less forgotten, but this much is certain that Lalo became a devoted follower of Guru Nanak from that very moment. Guru Nanak stayed with *Bhai* Lalo for a few days, and Mardana got leave to pay visit to his home at Talwandi, before going any further, for previously he had not left home with the intention of never returning again. While Mardana was away, Guru Nanak used to spend the day out in the country, so as not to disturb Lalo in his calling and return to Lalo's house in the evening, when he would teach his host the doctrines of his faith. But Mardana returned to Amenabad very soon, and with him brought an humble and earnest request from the old Rai Bular for at least one visit of the Guru to him in his old age. This request of his old friend Guru Nanak could not refuse. But it is said that Lalo did not like his so early departure from him, and even proposed to accompany him wherever he went, but Guru Nanak held out a hope to him that he would soon return to Amenabad and remain with him for fortnight more.

At Talwandi, Guru Nanak had a good many troubles. His parents and other relations all assembled to induce him to stay at home, and it was with great difficulty that he could get rid of them. All sorts dainties, silk cloths, horses and other articles of comfort, were named by his uncle, *Mehta* Lalu, which could be supplied to him at home; he was to have a free option to follow any profession – agriculture, business, trade or service or no profession at all; but Guru Nanak called all of them "poor pleasures" of this world, and told them in words which could not be mistaken that he had a higher and nobler mission to perform, and that a Higher Being had the control of his movements. When an appeal was made to him in the name of his relatives - mother, father, uncle, wife, children and friends of his youth, - Guru Nank as follows:-

"Forgiveness is my mother and contentment my father;

"Truth is my uncle, and with the help of these I have controlled my mind.

"Hear, O Lalu, this admonition, what are those relations who blind all to this world!

"Devotion, my brother, is with me, and True Love is my son;

"Endurance is my daughter, and in the company of these I enjoy myself;

"Meekness is friend to me, and purpose my retinue:

"This is all my family, with whom I ever reside.

"One God is my Master whi has created me,

"He who forsaketh him and seeketh another, "shall suffer pain, says Nanak."[27]

---

27 Rag Ramkulli, M.1, /vide Bala's *Janamsakhi*.
ਖਿਮਾ ਹਮਾਰੀ ਮਾਤਾ ਕਹੀਏ, ਸੰਤੋਖ ਹਮਾਰਾ ਪਿਤਾ,

Thus, said Guru Nanak, he could stay with them no longer. Regarding their last complaint as to "what would the people say about him, that he had deserted his parents and so on, he said:-

"O evolved beings of this world, how shall I save my honour?"
"If I speak, they would say, 'he chatters much.'
"If I be silent, they would say, 'he is a fool.'
"If I sit (at home), they would say, 'he is sitting on *suthur.'*
"If I go away, they would say, 'he has run away and put dust on the heads(of his elders).'
"If I be humble, they say, 'he is humble on account of fear.'
"In no way can I be safe from the people of this world, where may I pass my time without anxiety?
"Here (in the world) and there (in the next), the Creator alone will save my honour, says Nanak."[28]

ਸੱਤ ਹਮਾਰਾ ਚਾਚਾ ਕਹੀਏ, ਜਿਨ ਸੰਗ ਮਨੂਆ ਜਿੱਤਾ।
ਸੁਣ, ਲਾਲੂ, ਗੁਣ ਐਸਾ,
ਸਗਲੇ ਲੋਕ ਬੰਧਨ ਕੇ ਬਾਂਧੇ, ਸੋ ਗੁਣ ਨਹੀਏ ਕੈਸਾ ?
ਭਾਉ ਭਾਈ ਸੰਗ ਹਮਾਰੇ, ਪ੍ਰੇਮ ਪੁਤ ਸੋ ਸਾਚਾ,
ਧੀ ਹਮਾਰੀ ਧੀਰਜ ਬਣੀ, ਐਸੇ ਸੰਗ ਹਮ ਰਾਚਾ;
ਸ਼ਾਂਤ ਹਮਾਰੇ ਸੰਗ ਸਹੇਲੀ ਮਤਿ ਹਮਾਰੀ ਚੇਲੀ:
ਇਹ ਕੁੰਟਬ ਹਮਾਰਾ ਕਹੀਏ, ਸਾਸ ਸਾਸ ਸੰਗ ਖੇਲੀ।
ਏਕੰਕਾਰ ਹਮਾਰਾ ਖ਼ਾਵੰਦ, ਜਿਨ ਹਮ ਬਣਤ ਬਣਾਏ,
ਉਸ ਕੋ ਛਾਡ ਅਵਰ ਕੋ ਲਾਗੇ, ਨਾਨਕ ਸੋ ਦੁੱਖ ਪਾਏ।।
28 Shabd, M 1, Vide Bala's *Janamsakhi.*
ਏ ਸਕਲੀਓ ਪੰਜ ਭੀਤੀਓ, ਕਿਉਂਕਰ ਰੱਖਾਂ ਪੱਤ?
ਜਾ ਬੋਲਾਂ, ਤਾਂ ਆਖੀਏ, "ਬੜ ਬੜ ਕਰੇ ਬਹੁਤ";
ਚੁਪ ਕਰਾਂ, ਤਾਂ ਆਖੀਏ, "ਇਸ ਘਟ ਨਾਹੀ ਮੱਤ";
ਜੇ ਬਹਿ ਰਹਾਂ ਤਾਂ ਆਖੀਏ, "ਬੈਠਾ ਸੱਥਰ ਘੱਤ";
ਉਠ ਚਲਾਂ, ਤਾਂ ਆਖਦੇ, "ਛਾਰ ਗਿਆ ਸਿਰ ਘੱਤ";
ਜੇਕਰ ਨਿਵਾਂ, ਤਾਂ ਆਖੀਏ, "ਡਰਦਾ ਕਰੇ ਭਗੱਤ",
ਕਾਈ ਗਲੀ ਨਾ ਮੇਵਨੀ, ਕਿਤ ਵਲ ਕਢਾਂ ਝੱਤ;
ਏਥੇ, ਓਥੇ, ਨਾਨਕਾ, ਕਰਤਾ ਰਖੇ ਪੱਤ।।

Rai Bular was much pleased at the Guru's visit. He was going to bow down before his visitor, when the latter took hold of him, and asked him not to do so, as he was older than himself. After this, Guru Nanak taught him so many noble lessons and satisfied him on many a spiritual and religious topic. It is said that the first dinner served to him at the house of Rai Bular contained also a dish of meat. When Guru Nanak asked the Rai's permission to leave, the latter requested him to bid some service, to which Guru Nanak replied:-

"One service would I tell thee, if thou wouldst accept it."

"Where thy ownmight is of no avail, lay thy worship to Him most devoutly."[29]

On his return journey to Amenabad, Guru Nanak visited Lahore and Sialkot. At Lahore, he saw and talked to spiritual subjects to, Seid Ahmad Mir Taqi; and, at Sailkot, he baffled a Mussalman *faqir,* Hamza Gous by name, and told him not to be indignant at the world, as it was not inhabited solely by vile sort of people. There were also to be found in it men who may really be called servants of God; and even those who were followers of Satan had to be reclaimed to the Kingdom of Heaven and were not to be allowed to perish. As a practical way of convincing Hamza of the truth of the above, Nanak sent Mardana with a couple of pices to purchase for him "Truth and Falsehood" from the *bazar.* After sometime, Mardana returned with a piece of paper with inscription, "Death the Truth and Life the Falsehood" on it. On this Hamza Gous did not believe that the man who wrote the inscription could or does carry out this principle in practice. But when the writer, Mula by name, was called, he satisfied Hamza that the principle could be, and

---

29 Rag Srang, M. 1 Vide Bala's *Janamsakhi.*
ਹਿਕ ਡੁਰਮਾਇਸ਼ ਆਖੀਐ, ਜੇ ਮਨੇ ਸਾਂਈ:
ਜਿਸ ਤੇ ਜੋਰ ਨ ਚਲਈ, ਕਰ ਜੋਰ ਧਿਆਈ॥

was being, practiced by him. The place where Guru Nanak had stayed at Sailkot now bears the Grand Gurudwara, called the *Ber Sahib,* as the tree, under which he was sitting, is also very scrupulously preserved to this day.

At Amenabad, after his return, he had good many troubles. The people of the village did not allow him to live and do his works peacefully. He was everywhere derided and scoffed at as a "heretic" and Mardana was hooted as the "heretic's musician". *Mulik* Bhago, the grandee of the place, was offended with him for refusing to accept his invitation to a brahmbhoj, dinner given by him to all Brahmans and *Sadhus* at Amenabad, and for his public preference of *Bhai* Lalo's coarse bread to the dainties of the *Mulik,* on the ground that the former was earned by sheer dint of honest labour, and the latter by cruel exactions from the poor and helpless. *Mulik* Bhago and his satellites made it hard for him and his disciples to live there in peace. But amid all these persecutions was heard the bold and undaunted voice which could not be mistaken: "Mardana, Fear Not. The World Is Foolish And Will Turn To Thee After Groveling In The Dust For Ages!" Prophetic and forcible as these words were, they could not but have a most salutary effect upon their hearer. *Mardana never left Guru Nanak's company after this, till his death.*

Before leaving Amenabad Guru Nanak established there a *Manji* (Cot)[30] and put it in charge of the carpenter-disciple. It seems that having had the idea of establishing these *Manjis,* even before his start, Guru Nanak must have purposely returned to, and stayed at Amenabad, to educate *Bhai* Lalo in his doctrines and principles, in order to enable him to carry on preaching work there after his departure. Otherwise, the mere wish of a Sikh, it may be remarked,

---

30 Church or Chapel ; so called because the bishop or the head of the Chapel, the *Baba* (Father), as he was called, used to sit on a cot, while his followers and audience had to squat on the floor. Guru Nanak established a number of similar chapols in different parts of southern Asia.

although sometimes a sufficient excuse, could r
warrant for one, who had taken up to himself so
heavy duties, to while away so much of his pre
one place.

On leaving Amenabad, Guru Nanak visited many places in
the Punjab, and then left for Mecca, via Bushehr. In the west,
he visited Mecca, Medina and other important places. It also
appears that he visited Stamboul a story being related of his
interview "with the Sultan of Turkey, who was noted for his
cupidity and his extreme oppression of his subjects. Nanak's
admonitions had a great effect on the Sultan, who is said to
have bestowed his horded treasures on the *faqirs* and the needy,
and to have discontinued his tyranny over his people."[31]His
return from the west seems to have been via Baghdad, Kandhar
and Kabul. In many of these places, and notably at Bushahr
and Kabul, he seems to have established *Manjis* as some of the
*Janamsakhi*s give indications of his having done so.[32]

After visiting the western places, Guru Nanak returned to
the Punjab and made a tour in the east and the south. He visited
Kurukshetra, Hardwar, Jaggannath, and other sacred places of
the Hindus, at each place of which he had discussions with the
Brahmans *Pundit*s and monks of various orders, a few of which
will be described in the next chapter. Having been to Siam and
Burma, he went to the Deccan and to Ceylon. Raja Shiv Nabh

---

31 Mr. Muhammad Latif's history of Pujnab Page 245. But I have not
   been able to trace the source where Mr. Muhammad Latif has got his
   information on this points.

32 If there Masjis do not exist there now it is probably due to the inter-
   communication between these western cities and the Punjab having been
   mainly discontinued after Guru Nanak, So for as the sikh movement was
   concerned. No other Guru ever afterwards visited any of these places
   and therefore the mission of Guru Nanak in the west seems to have
   come to a standstill and probably to an ultimate extinction for want of
   any cohesive force. People for Kabul alone of all the towns went to the
   Punjab are described to have visited occasionally the successors of Guru
   Nanak and in Kabul therefore Guru Nanak's mission still survives in its
   rudimentary form.

ı Ceylon is said to have become his Sikh, and to him Guru Nanak (is said to have) addressed a lesson contained in the Pransangli, a book no longer extant.

Some *shabds* are also pointed out in the *Granth Sahib* as having been uttered in Ceylon, which contain lessons to the Raja and other members of his family. In the Deccan, he visited, among other places, Surat, where he had a discussion with the *Jains*; and then he returned to the Punjab via Sindh. His mission seems to have got a deeper root in Sindh than in the Deccan, Bengal or Burma, probably on account of its closer proximity to the Punjab; or perhaps the fact is that he spent more time in Sindh than in either of the southern and eastern countries. From Sindh he also appears to have paid another visit to Bawa Wali at Kandhar, whose acquaintance he had first made at Hassanabdal, in the Rawalpindi district. It was on his return from this journey that, at a place called Khawarzim, his companion, Mardana, died.

Therefore he visited Talwandi once more and took with him Sajada, son of Mardana. At Talwandi he was also told of the deaths of his own father and mother in his absence. After leaving Talwandi, Sajada expressed the desire of seeing his father's death place, so he was commissioned to go to the west and set up a *Manji* at the tomb of his father. For this purpose, Sajada was duly instructed and initiated into the teachings of the Guru. Guru Nanak then again visited Sultanpore, as he had done twice or thrice before while touring in the Punjab, and saw his sister. After this, he visited Ferozpore, Pakpatan, Mithankot, Multan and other places, and then Thanesar &c.

At this time, at least in the Punjab, he had made a fair progress in his mission which was gradually gaining ground amongst the masses. A visit to Delhi ended in his imprisonment in jail. At the time of Baber's conquest, he was released by the victorious monarch. Details of this incident will be given in the next chapter. On his return from Delhi after his release, he remained for some time, at Pakhoke, his father-in-law's village, and then in about 1530 of the Christian era he finally settled at Kartarpore, on the Ravi, founded by himself. He sent for his family to Kartarpore and here he used to receive visitors from outstations.

From Kartarpore he seems to have paid a visit to Kashmere and other hill stations in the Himalayas, and, after another visit to Hardwar at the end of this tour, he returned to Kartarpore, to leave it no more.

In the above narrative of Guru Nanak's travels, only those places have been mentioned which are of great note, otherwise there is a multitude of other places where he preached to, and converted, the people, but which could not be noted in this narrative without fear of historical inaccuracy; because information about them was not sure and authentic. Some places he visited many times, e.g., Amenabad, but this has not been particularly noted. His travels cover a period of about thirty years, and the settlement of Kartarpore seems to have been founded by him about the Christian year, 1530.

CR80

CHAPTER 7
A FEW ANECDOTES FROM HIS TRAVELS

1 *Yogis* At Nanakmata

At Nanakmata, then called Gorakhmata, he had a very lengthy and hot contest with the *yogis*.[33] The whole discussion, called the *Sidhgoshta* (conversation with the *siddha* and *yogis*), is preserved in the *Granth Sahib* and is very interesting. But before the *Sidhgosht* took place, an attempt was made by the *yogis* to induce Nanak to join their order. As soon as he was accosted by the *peer* (the head of the convent of these monks) with "*adesh, adesh* of Gorakh Nath, *adesh* of 84

---

33 An order of monks founded by Gorakh Nath and followed by 84 sidhs(mendicants supposed to possess supernatural powers) These monks make a long cut through the labe of their ears in which they ears large rings of various materials – wood, glass, silver, gold called mundran. They put on other various symbols rub ashes on their body, shave their heads clean and blow horn and hold a prop in their hands. They generally live outside habitation and occasionally travel in distant lands and go to pilgrimage to holy places. The monks of this order take all sorts of intoxicants, smoke tobacco and opium and eat flesh. They are very zealous to convert others to their order. Their salutation is *Adesh* (ਆਦੇਸ਼), literally meaning order or command. It is the command of the founders of their order that they remind in their salutation

sidhs," Guru Nanak replied, "Yea *adesh* of the Primeval Being!" After this salutation, there was a brief friendly conversation, in the course of which the *peer* proposed to Guru Nanak to join his order and wear the symbols prescribed therefore. Guru Nanak's reply was in the following strain:

"*Yog* is not the *khinta* (ragged garment), *yog* is not the *danda* (staff) and *yog* is not the rubbing of ashes.

"*Yog* is not the clean shaving of head and *yog* is not the blowing of horn."

"The means of *yog*[34] can only be obtained if you live passionless (unstained) amidst passion.

"*Yog* cannot be obtained by words.

"*Yogi* is he who looks upon all with an equal eye.

"*Yog* does not consist in living in a graveyard or crematorium, and *yog* does not lie in sitting with eyes closed.

"*Yog* does not consist in travelling in foreign lands, and *yog* is not the bathing at holy places.

"The means of *yog* can only be obtained by living passionless amidst passions."[35]

This lengthy sermon was followed by a battle of words and miracles, in which the *Janamsakhi*s are unanimous in giving the palm of superiority of Guru Nanak. His direct answers baffled the *yogis*, and from that day forth the place is known as Nanakmata, rather than Gorakhmata.

---

34 Yog literally means union, hence Union with God.
35 Rag Suhi, M. 1 Sh. 8

ਜੋਗੁ ਨ ਖਿੰਬਾ, ਜੋਗੁ ਨ ਡੰਡੈ, ਜੋਗੁ ਨ ਭਸਮ ਚੜਾਈਐ।
ਜੋਗਨ ਮੁੰਦੀ ਮੂੰਡ ਮੁੰਡਾਈਐ ਜੋਗੁ ਨ ਸਿੰਦੀ ਵਾਈਐ।
ਅੰਜਨ ਮਾਹੀ ਨਿਰੰਜਨ ਰਹੀਐ, ਜੋਗ ਜੁਗਤਿ ਇਵ ਪਾਈਐ।
ਗਲੀ ਜੋਗੁਨ ਹੋਈ,
ਏਕ ਦ੍ਰਿਸ਼ਟਿ ਕਰਿ, ਸਮਸਰਿ ਜਾਣੈ ਜੋਗੀ ਕਹੀਐ ਸੋਈ।
ਜੋਗੁ ਨ ਬਾਹਰਿ ਮੜੀ ਮਸਾਣੀ, ਜੋਗੁ ਨਟਾੜੀ ਲਾਈਐ।
ਜੋਗੁ ਨ ਦੇਸਿ ਦਿਸੰਤਰ ਭਵੀਐ, ਜੋਗੁ ਨ ਤੀਰਥ ਨਾਈਐ।
ਅੰਜਨ ਮਾਹਿ ਨਿਰੰਜਨ ਰਹੀਐ, ਜੋਗ ਜੁਗਤ ਇਵ ਪਾਈਐ।

2 The *Punja Sahib*

At Hassanabdal, in the district of Rawalpindi, he had a dispute with Bawa Wali of Kandhar. Bawa Wali's place of abode was at the top of a small hillock overlooking the village. Guru Nanak stayed at the foot of the hill in close proximity to the village. Legend says that Mardana was sent by Guru Nanak up the hill to fetch a pail of water for him, for pure water could not be had in the plains below. As Mardana approached the pool with his basin, Bawa wali noticed his stranger's appearance and enquired who he was. Mardana told him all about himself and his master, and also advised Wali to come and visit his master who was a great Prophet of God. Wali got offended at this and did not allow Mardana to take water from the pool. He told him, if his master was such a prophet, he ought not to send for water from others' abodes. Guru Nanak sent Mardana back, saying that he was but a poor creature of God and did not lay any claims to being a Prophet, but Wali was not moved. In the end, Guru Nanak was compelled to bore a small hole near the place where he was sitting, and lo! a stream of water rushed forth out of it. It is said that Wali's pool dried up simultaneously, as the same water had flowed out of the hole down the hill. Wali got still more offended and hurled the hill down upon Nanak's head. Nanak, *daton*[36] in hand, was cleansing his mouth, when he saw the mountain's precipitous advance. He quietly raised his free right arm in defence. The hill touched his hand and stood still! An impression of the palm of the hand was left on the side of the hill, which it still bears, and is known as the *"Punja Sahib,"* and is, and shall ever be an object of reverence for the Sikhs. The flow of water also increased at the same time and continues to this day. Mr. Muhammad Latif simply mentions that Nanak "is said, by interposing his hand, to have prevented a landslip. The hill received the impression of Nanak's hand, which exists to this day, and the place is called *Punja Sahib*." But he does not refer to the Muhammadan *faqir* and the story told above. Whatever the

---

36 A small green stick used as tooth brush

nature of the story may be, and it is quite probable that it is true, it is nevertheless certain that the followers of Guru Nanak did not, and do not, hesitate to ascribe to him supernatural powers.

3 Kurukshetra

When he was at Kurukshetra, the Hindus had assembled there in large numbers from all parts of the Hindustan to enjoy the grand *Kumbhi mela* or *Surya grihin,* Eclipse of the Sun. There, he saw thousands upon thousands of people, sunk into the depths of ignorance, under the innocent belief that by offering prayers and giving alms they could win the merit of getting Sun's release from the dreadful jaws of the terrible and offended Rahu who was eating it up. This was a splendid opportunity for the Brahmans. The *mela* was in full swing when Guru Nanak reached there, and with a purpose. Nanak saw this and his heart burnt within him. Whether he himself explained the correct and exact idea of what caused the eclipse, is not certain, for the *Janamsakhi*s do not mention his having done so, but he was sure that these phenomena of the Universe were out of human control, and that their prayers and alms notwithstanding, year after year, the sun was, and would still be, similarly eclipsed at the proper hour. Nanak was anxious to raise the ignorant people from their degraded condition. He caught a fish from the pool, put it into a kettle and began to cook it. It is objectionable to eat meat, according to the orthodox Hindus, but on a *purbi* occasion, no Hindu however fond of meat he may be, would even think of that article. The very idea is quite reprehensible and is sufficient to justify the excommunication of at least the individual, if not also of the whole of his family, from the community. When people saw Nanak cooking fish, general excitement prevailed. The more indignant of them took cudgels in hands and ran upon him furiously. But Guru Nanak pacified them in his usual humble and eloquent way, and said he had done nothing wrong. Why should they detest flesh when they themselves were made of it. Having given a satisfactory, but not generally acceptable, explanation of his conduct, and having been asked by some one present as to who he was and what his caste and name, he said, "Why harp upon caste and name, when all have the same Protector? Whoever calls himself good, will only be so if he is honoured in the presence of the Almighty God."[37] After this he at once launched forth into his sermon, and began to preach to the audience that had assembled there. Among other matters, he dwelt upon their practice of giving alms to Brahmans, on that occasion in the vain hope of thereby benefitting their ancestors and the Sun. By so many devices, fair and foul, he said, do they amass their wealth, and on occasions like that, when nature repeats her phenomena, they bestow it on the Brahmans, in the vain hope that it will benefit their ancestors. Even supposing for a moment that these gifts would reaches them, shall not the ancestors be arrested as swindlers, when things, earned by foul means and given in their names, are recognised by others ? Ah! Don't be foolish, O people. These things shall not benefit them. Come and worship Him who is the Maintainer of all. Your ancestors do not depend on your gifts. They have to reap what they have sown here when alive. If you have earned money by honest labour and given it in charity to the poor, that will no doubt benefit ye; but not this ignorant practice[38]. Strange to say that, at the very first sight of him, all active opposition had vanished, and

---

37 *Var* Sri Rag, M. 1 *Shlok* 3 (1)

ਫਕੜ ਜਾਤੀ ਫਕੜੁ ਨਾਉ;
ਸਭਨਾਂ ਜੀਆਂ ਇਕਾ ਛਾਉ।
ਆਪਹੁ ਜੇਕੋ ਭਲਾ ਕਹਾਏ,
ਨਾਨਕ, ਤਾਂ ਪਰੁ ਜਾਪੈ, ਜਾਂ ਪਤਿ ਲੇਖੇ ਪਾਏ।।

38 Asa di VAr, M.1, *Shlok* 17(1)

ਜੇ ਮੋਹਾਕਾ ਘਰੁ ਮੁਹੈ, ਘਰ ਮੁਹਿ, ਪਿਤ੍ਰੀ ਦੇਇ;
ਅਗੇ ਵਸਤੁ ਸਿਞਾਣੀਐ, ਪਿਤ੍ਰੀ ਚੋਰ ਕਰੇਇ;
ਵਢੀਅਹਿ ਹਥ ਦਲਾਲ ਕੇ. ਮੁਸਫੀ ਏਹ ਕਰੇਇ;
ਨਾਨਕ ਅਗੈ ਸੋ ਮਿਲੈ, ਜਿ ਖਟੇ, ਘਾਲੇ, ਦੇਇ।।

the spirit with which the assailants had come to drive him out of the *mela* was quite cooled down in his holy presence. His appearance inspired love in people's hearts, and such was the effect of his sermon that good many people followed him and were converted to his faith. A *Manji* was established there and Guru Nanak then resumed his travels.

4 Mecca

When Nanak visited Mecca and Medina, he had very interesting discussions with the *Mullahs* and Kazis. The incident at Mecca is specially noteworthy. Guru Nanak reached there in the evening and was dressed in blue, after the fashion of Hajis, and held a stick in hand, a book under arm and had also equipped himself with a prayer-carpet and a water-jug. Thus furnished, he slept with his feet towards the *Kaaba*. The Imams and others, when they saw him, got enraged, and began to swear at him, "Who the *kafir*, lying with his feet towards the House of God"? said one, Jiwan, giving him a kick at the same time. "Pray be not furious," said Guru Nanak, "I have come from afar, and was tired and weary; so I have thrown myself here. *Turn my feet to where the House of God is not!*" Legend says that, as soon as the pilgrims took hold of his feet, their hearts palpitated with emotions and a carrent of delight passed through their veins. They turned the feet to different directions, but lo! the *Kaaba* also went round and round. This may be an allegorical way of showing that such was the effect of Guru Nanak's words that those present were spell-bound, and thenceforward began to believe that the House of God was not only in the *Kaaba* but on all sides.

On this, many of those present prostrated themselves before Nanak, and questioned him as to whence he had come. On learning that Nanak had come from Hindustan, the next question put to him was whether he was a Hindu or Mussalman. Guru Nanak's reply to this vexed question was that he was neither but that his body was made of 5 elements and was mysteriously playing about. "Well, who is better of two, Hindu or Mussalman?" asked the questioner. *Baba* said, 'O Hajis, both shall weep without good deeds, and shall not obtain rest in the Kingdom of Heaven. Light is the dye of *kusumbha* and cannot remain fast on washing. Both revile each other; where is the room for Ram (God) or Rahim (God) to stand amongst them. The world is thus following the ways of Satan."[39]

5 Brindaban

In Brindaban he witnessed the Krishna-leela (the performance of Krishna), and got excited at the profane representation of God in the body of Krishna. Krishna flirting with milk-maids, called *gopees*, Krishna killing Kans and *Kali* Nag, were spectacles revolting to all sense of holiness and decency and spirituality. But then, calling such a hero by the epithet of God was what Guru Nanak's enthusiastic and pure and spiritual heart could not endure. He at once broke forth and addressed the people thus:-

> The followers play, and leaders dance,
>   Shake their feet and roll their heads.
> Dust[40] fileth and falleth on their hair,
>   The spectators seeing it laugh and go home.
> For the sake of food the performers beat time,
>   And dash themselves on the ground.

---

39 *Vars* of *Bhai* Gurdas Ji, 1 (33).
ਪੁਛਣ ਗਲ ਈਮਾਨ ਦੀ ਕਾਜ਼ੀ ਮੁਲਾਂ ਇਕਠੇ ਹੋਈ;
ਵਡਾ ਸਾਂਗ ਵਰਤਾਇਆ ਲਖ ਨ ਸਕੈ ਕੁਦਰਤਿ ਕੋਈ।
ਪੁਛਣ ਖੋਲ ਕਿਤਾਬ ਨੂ ਵਡਾ ਹਿੰਦੂ ਕਿ ਮੁਸਲਮਾਨੋਈ ?
ਬਾਬਾ ਆਖੇ ਹਾਜੀਆ, ਸ਼ੁਭ ਅਮਲਾਂ ਬਾਝੋਂ ਦੇਵੇ ਰੋਈ,
ਹਿੰਦੂ ਮੁਸਲਮਾਨ ਦੋਇ ਦਰਗਹਿ ਅੰਦਰ ਲੈਨ ਨ ਢੋਈ।
ਕੱਚਾ ਰੰਗ ਕੁਸਭ ਕਾ ਪਾਣੀ ਧੋਤੇ ਥਿਰ ਨ ਰਹੋਈ;
ਕਰਨ ਬਖੀਲੀ ਆਪ ਵਿਚ, ਰਾਮ ਰਹੀਮਕ ਥਾਇ ਖਲੋਈ ?
ਰਾਹ ਸ਼ੈਤਾਨੀ ਦੁਨੀਆਂ ਗੋਈ॥

40 In India they did not use to have proper stages for the performance of dramas, Therefore, whenever they acted they did so on bare ground and hence the dust.

The milk-maids sing, Krishnas sing,
Sitas and royal Ramas sing,
(But mind), Formless is the Fearless One, whose Name is True.
And whose creation is the whole Universe.[41]

Then he went on to tell them that "dancing ad jumping were recreations of the mind." "Every one danceth according to his own acts. But those who dance and laugh shall weep on their departure; they cannot fly away or obtain supernatural powers," so as to escape death. These their acts could not denote their love of God, neither could this conduct make them God-fearing. "Fear and Love co-exist in sincere hearts." Then followed a discussion between the chief *Pundit* (the stage manager) and Guru Nanak, as to the Divine character of Krishna and Rama. The gist of Guru Nanak's opinion on this point appears in the following hymns:-

How can Thy greatness be sung, O Lord?
Thou pervades and givest light to all.
Thou hast created air and established the whole earth
therein and hast arranged water and fire.
The Ten-headed[42] one (Ravan) was blind to get his
neck cut off; (otherwise) what greatness was
achieved in the killing of Ravan ?

---

41 Asa di *Var Shlok* 5(2)
ਵਾਇਨ ਚੇਲੇ, ਨਚਨ ਗੁਰ, ਪੈਰ ਹਲਾਇਨ, ਫੇਰਨ ਸਿਰ।
ਉਡ ਉਡ ਰਾਵਾ ਝਾਟੇ ਪਾਇ। ਵੇਖੇ ਲੋਕ ਹਸੇ ਘਰ ਜਾਇ।
ਰੋਟੀਆਂ ਕਾਰਨ ਪੂਰੇ ਤਾਲ, ਆਪ ਪਛਾੜਹਿ ਧਰਤੀ ਨਾਲ।
ਗਾਵਨ ਗੋਪੀਆਂ ਗਾਵਨ ਕਾਨ। ਗਾਵਨ ਸੀਤਾ, ਰਾਜੇ ਰਾਮ।
ਨਿਰਭਉ ਨਿਰੰਕਾਰ ਸਚ ਨਾਮਾਜਾਕਾਕੀਆ ਸਗਲ ਜਹਾਨ॥

42 Ravan, Raja of Ceylon is said to have got ten heads on this neck. He was killed by Rama who is therefore believed to have been an incarnation of God. The point here is that God is the creator of all the elements then why sing of him as killer of Ravan who was in face blinded by his passions and had thus lost his life. Is He great because Rama Killed Ravan?

Thou, having created the living beings, hast retained
their destinies in Thy own hands ; then what
greatness has been achieved by the killer of *Kali*?[43]

Whose husband shouldst Thou be called and who
Thy wife ? Thou art present in all.
Brahma, the giver of blessings, with all his family
and descerulants, went out to investigate Thy Universe;
But could not find its limit (then) what greatness
in slaying Kans[44]
Thou created the *ratans* (gems); others were astray to think
that *they* obtained them by churning the oceans.[45]
Nanak says, how couldst Thou be concealed by hiding?
Yet they divide Thee in several parts. [46]

Then followed the following *shabd* as to how should one dance
to the Lord of the Universe:

Let His praise be the full Chimes!
All other dancing produces no pleasure.

---

43 Kali was a large dreadful Cobra, believed to have been killed by Krishna
44 Kans maternal uncle of Krishna, was a cruel heartless monarch who was
killed by his nephew.
45 It is believed that Vishnu churned the ocean and got 14 ratans out of
them.
46 Rag Asa, M.1, Sh 2(7).

ਕਿਆ ਉਪਮਾ ਤੇਰੀ ਆਖੀ ਜਾਇ ?
ਤੂ ਸਰਬੇ ਮਹਿ ਰਹਿਆ ਲਿਵ ਲਾਇ।
ਪਉਨ ਉਪਾਇ ਧਰੀ ਸਭ ਧਰਤੀ, ਜਲ ਅਗਨੀ ਕਾ ਬੰਧ ਕੀਆ,
ਅੰਧੁਲੇ ਦਹਿਸਿਰ ਮੁੰਡ ਕਟਾਇਆ, ਰਾਵਣ ਮਾਰ ਕਿਆ ਵਡਾ ਭਇਆ ?
ਜੀਉ ਉਪਾਇ ਜੁਗਤ ਹਥ ਕੀਨੀ, ਕਾਲੀ ਨਥ ਕਿਆ ਵਡਾ ਭਇਆ ?
ਕਿਸ ਤੁ ਪੁਰਖ ਜੋਰੁ ਕਉਣ ਕਹੀਐ, ਸਰਬ ਨਿਰੰਤਰ ਰਵ ਰਹਿਆ।
ਨਾਲ ਕੁਟੰਬ ਸਾਥੁ ਵਰਦਾਤਾ ਬ੍ਰਹਮਾ ਭਾਲਨ ਸ੍ਰਿਸ੍ਟਿਗਇਆ।
ਆਗੋ ਅੰਤ ਨ ਪਾਇਓ ਤਾਂਕਾ, ਕੰਸ ਛੇਦ ਕਿਆ ਵਡਾ ਭਇਆ ?
ਰਤਨ ਉਪਾਇ, ਧਰੇ ਖੀਰ ਮਥਿਆ, ਹੋਰ ਭਖਲਾਇ, ਜਿ ਅਸੀ ਕੀਆ।
ਕਹੇ ਨਾਨਕ ਛਪੇ ਕਿਉ ਛਪਿਆ, ਏਕੀ ਏਕੀ ਵੰਡਦੀਆ।।

Let veneration be the instrument and devotion the tambourine,
And to win joy and pleasure in the mind
Perform this devotion and this services:
And keep time in such dancing.

Let truth and contentment be the two cymbals
And felicity the musical instrument of the feet.
Let thy melody be distinguished by absence of love
      for the second one:
And keep time in such dancing.

Let thy turning round be fear of God,
Ever and always, while sitting and while rising;
Let thy reclining (in dance) be thy humility:
And keep time in such dancing.

Let such disciples be initiated into assembly,
As love to hear Gods' True Name from the Guru:
Nanak says again and again
Keep time in such dancing.[47]

---

47 Rag Asa, M. 1 Sh 2(6).
ਪੂਰੇ ਤਾਲ ਜਾਨੇ ਸਾਲਾਹਿ। ਹੋਰ ਨਚਣਾ ਖੁਸ਼ੀਆਂ ਮਨ ਮਾਹਿ।
ਵਾਜਾ ਪਤ. ਪਖਾਵਜ ਭਾਉ, ਹੋਈ ਅਨੰਦ ਸਦਾ ਮਨ ਚਾਉ,
ਏਹਾ ਭਗਤ ਏਹਾ ਤਪਤਾਉ;
      ਇਤ ਰੰਗ ਨਚਾਓ ਰਖ ਰਖ ਪਾਓ।
ਸਤਿ ਸੰਤੋਖੁ ਵਜਹਿ ਦੁਇ ਤਾਲ;ਪੈਰੀ ਵਾਜਾ ਸਦਾਨਿਹਾਲ;
ਰਾਗਾ ਨਾਦ ਨਹੀਂ ਦੂਜਾ ਭਾਉ;
      ਇਤ ਰੰਗ ਨਚਾਓ ਰਖ ਰਖ ਪਾਓ।
ਭਉ ਫੇਰੀ ਹੋਵੇ ਮਨ ਚੀਤ, ਬੇਹਦਿਆ ਉਠਦਿਆਂ ਨਿਤਾਨੀਤ;
ਲੇਟਣ ਲੇਟ ਜਾਨੇ ਤਨ ਸੁਆਹੁ:
      ਇਤ ਰੰਗ ਨਚਾਓ ਰਖ ਰਖ ਪਾਓ।
ਸਿਖ ਸਭਾ ਦੀਖਿਆ ਕਾ ਭਾਉ, ਗੁਰਮੁਖ ਸੁਣਨਾ ਸਾਚਾ ਨਾਓ।
ਨਾਨਕ ਆਖੇ ਵੇਰਾ ਵੇਰ:
      ਇਤ ਰੰਗ ਨਾਚਉ ਰਖ ਰਖ ਪੈਰ।।

A FEW ANECDOTES FROM HIS TRAVELS

6 Hardwar (First Visit)

During his first visit to Hardwar he seems to have had a discussion with *Byragis*[48] and *Sannyasees* who always used to quarrel over the right of precedence in ceremonials at the Ganges. Though both of these orders may have had a worthy origin, they were surely no longer what they may have been originally. All that had remained of them was their distinctive garbs and symbols, and a great hankering after means conductive to their obtaining personal superiority over others, though not preserved by them. They exacted respect and presents from the "men of the world." Otherwise, whatever vices assail and trouble these latter, were in no way powerless before them; because devoid of any fear of a *biradri* (caste-fellows), that great check which the observance of caste has put on worldly men, and devoid of any legitimate means to satisfy their natural passions, these men succumbed to the foul temptation and vices, perhaps more recklessly. Begging had become their sole outward occupation, and fear or knowledge of God and faith in, or love for, Him had no longer a place in their hearts. This condition of theirs was boldly exposed by Guru Nanak, and many of them were forced to acknowledge their weaknesses, if not openly, at least in their hearts.

"You colour your clothes to adopt the garb of your order," said he to the *Sannyasees*, "and wear a *khintha* of worn out cloth and also a bag to receive alms in, and you got abegging from door to door and cheat the world, thus losing all respect, O ye blind fellows! You are thus lost in absurd superstition and are thus wasting your lives for nothing." "You leave your own wives behind you," he continued to tell them, "but, controlled by passions, you go after other women. Blessed is he, whose mind is attached to the feet of the Lord, be he a house-holder, a *Sanyasee* or a *Yogi*".[49]

---

48 Orders Of Monks
49 Rag Maru, M.1, Asht *Shlok* 7(2).
ਘੋਲੀ ਗੇਰੂ ਰੰਗ ਚੜ੍ਹਾਇਆ ਵਸਤ ਭੇਖ ਭੇਖਾਰੀ।
ਕਾਪੜ ਫਾੜਿ ਬਨਾਈ ਖਿੰਥਾਝੋਲੀ ਮਾਇਆ ਧਾਰੀ।

7 Benares At Benares he had many an engagement

with Brahmans and *Pundit*s. With one Brahman he had a discussion about observing caste in eating and drinking. The Brahman did not like Guru Nanak's eating the food prepared and offered by every and any honest and loving man, and when he expressed his sentiments to Guru Nanak, the latter, after telling him that if he were to be strict in observing these superstitious practices in eating and drinking, he could never be pure, told him that profaneness consisted not of eating food prepared by another or outside the circumstances of *chauka*, but of one's own bad actions. "Evil conscience is a *dumni*, misplaced mercy the butcher's woman, backbiting is the sweeper-woman and anger is the *chandal*: these four are always living with thee, what use then in drawing a line around thyself? On the other hand, draw the circumstances of deeds of truth and contentment (around thee) and (sit therein after having had a) bath of remembering God's Name; for those alone are blessed in the Kingdom of Heaven who do not indulge in sins."[50] "Thy mind, thy body, thy tongue and thy mouth, all become profane by telling a lie, how canst then thou be pure?"[51]

ਘਰ ਘਰ ਮਾਂਗੇ ਜਗ ਪੁਬੋਧੇ ਮਨ ਅੰਧਿ ਪਤਿ ਹਾਰੀ।।
ਭਰਮ ਭੁਲਾਣਾ ਸ਼ਬਦੁ ਨ ਚੀਨੈ ਜੂਐ ਬਾਜੀ ਹਾਰੀ।
ਇਸਤੁੀ ਤਜ ਕਰ ਕਾਮ ਵਧਾਇਆ ਚਿਤ ਲਾਇਆ ਪਰਨਾਰੀ।
ਧਨ ਗਿਰਹੀ ਸੰਨਿਆਸੀ ਜੋਗੀ ਜਿਹੇਰ ਚਰਣੀ ਚਿਤ ਲਾਇ।

50 *Var* sri Rag *Shlok* M, 1 20 (1).

ਕਬੁਧ ਡੂਮਣੀ ਕੁਦਇਆ ਕਸਾਇਨ, ਪਰਨਿੰਦਾ ਘਟ
ਚੁਹੜੀ ਮੁਠੀ ਕ੍ਰੋਧ ਚੰਡਾਲਿ।
ਕਾਰੀ ਕਢੀ ਕਿਆ ਥੀਐ ਜਾ ਚਾਰੇ ਬੈਠੀਆਂ ਨਾਲ।
ਸਚੁ ਸੰਜਮ ਕਰਨੀ ਕਾਰਾ ਲਾਵਨ ਨਾਉ ਜਪੇਈ।
ਨਾਨਕ ਅਗੋ ਉਤਮ ਸੇਇ ਜੇ ਪਾਪਾਂ ਪਧਿ ਨ ਦੇਈ।

51 Sri Rag, M. 1 Asht, *Shlok* 5(1).

ਮਨ ਜੂਠਾ, ਤਨੁ ਜੂਠਾ ਹੈ, ਜੇਹਵਾ ਜੂਠੀ ਹੋਇ,
ਮੁਖ ਜੂਠੈ, ਝੂਠ ਬੋਲਨਾ, ਕਿਉਕਰ ਸੁਚਾ ਹੋਇ,

After this there was a discussion with one *Pundit*, named Chattar Dass, on idol-worship. It will be needless to dwell here on all his sayings, which were uttered on this occasion, nor is it easy to testify as to the absolute correctness of all the details given of this debate. Suffice it to say, that his open, straightforward and bold arguments appealed direct to the people and his opponent, and they at once acknowledged that their theory of "Ancient practice," based on the texts of Narad and other *Purans,* was quite an absurd one. "Rather wash your own minds than wash and worship the bodies of these stones images, and remove filth from your minds and obtain salvation."[52]

He had similar engagements with a number of other people belonging to different ascetic orders. The *Pundits*, the *Nangas* (naked), the Fruit-eaters, the Forest-dwellers, the Silents, and others, all had each their share when they tried to defeat and convert Nanak to their own respective orders. But, on the other hand, they themselves were defeated and converted by Guru Nanak.

8 Jaggannath

At Jaggannath (Puri), he visited the temple of Sri Krishna one day at dusk in the evening. The *Pujarees* (priests) were busy in performing the *Arti* worship of the idols. This they did by means of a large golden salver, enchased with pearls, and fitted in the center with a lamp made of the same metal, in which burnt a number of wicks, fed with *ghee*, and also supplied with burning incense, rice, flowers, sweets, saffron water, and other similar articles. The High Priest held the salver, which was a sort of candelabrum, in his hands and was giving it, quite respectfully, constant flourishes in front of idol, while all were chanting songs in its praise, beating drums, sounding instruments and sprinkling rice, flowers and saffron water over, and presenting

---

52 Rag Goojri M. 1, Sh. 1(2).
ਬਾਹਿਰ ਦੇਵ ਪਖਾਲੀਅਹਿ ਜੇ ਮਨਿ ਧੋਵਹਿ ਕੋਇ।
ਜੂਠ ਲਹੈ ਜੀਉ ਮਾਜੀਐ ਮੋਖ ਪਿਆਲਾ ਹੋਇ।

sweets to it. While they were thus engaged, Guru Nanak stepped in and seated himself aside to watch their proceedings. When they had finished, one of them asked Guru Nanak why he had not stood up and joined in the *Arti* worship of "Thakur ji"(the Lord). *"Arti* Worship? Of the Lord? Oh, yours was not the proper worship of the Lord! My Lord's *Arti* is ever and anon being performed, night and day, here and there".

"Your Thakurji's *Arti?* Where it is? asked the High Priest. "You must be and atheist," said he, "to hold aloof from this Holy Service of Sri Krishna Bhagwan." On this Guru Nanak uttered the following hymn in praise of the Lord of the Universe:--

The firmament is Thy salver, O Lord; the orbs of the stars, the
   pearls enchased in it; the sun and the moon are thy lamp.

The whole perfume is Thy incense; the wind fans
   Thee; the whole vegetable kingdom are
   Thy flowers, O Lord of Light!

How fine is the *Arti* ! O Destroyer of fear;
Unbeaten strains of ecstasy sound for trumpets.

Thou hast a thousand eyes, yet not one eye; Thou hast a
   thousand forms, yet not one form;
Thou hast a thousand stainless feet yet not one foot;
   Thou hast a thousand organs of smell, yet not one organ;
   I marvel at this play of Thine!

The Light which is in everything, is Thine, O Lord of Light!
From its brilliancy everything is brilliant.
By the Guru's teaching the Light becometh manifest.
That which pleaseth Thee is Thy real *Arti.*

O God! my mind is fascinated with the essence of
   Thy Lotus feet;[53] night and day I thirst for it.

---

53 These has the idea of extreme love and respect for the Lord. Nanak always
   looks upon the feet out of great veneration for Him.

Give the water of Thy favour to the *sarang*, Nanak so that he may rest contented in Thy Name.[54]

9 Imprisonment at Delhi

At first the Hindus and the Muhammadans had attached little importance to what Guru Nanak said and taught, but when the agitation increased and the number of his followers began to multiply, they were all alarmed. Both united to report the matter to the Delhi Durbar. Free use was made of exaggeration and misrepresentation, as is not unfrequently the case in an oriental Durbar. That religious bigotry and fanaticism which characterised, with few rare and honourable exceptions, the Muhammadan rule in Hindustan, was at its highest during the reign of the Lodhi dynasty, and Sultan Ibrahim was perhaps the worst of his tribe. Toleration was quite unknown during his reign. Guru Nanak was arrested on a charge of heresy and was brought to the Durbar Hall, on entering which he uttered only his usual salutation of Sat Kartar, "True is the Creator". That offended the Sultan still more, and a brief altercation followed, during the course of which Guru Nanak openly denied the mediation of Muhammad or Rama for the salvation of human

---

54 Rag Dhanasri, M. 1, *Arti* Sh.9.

ਗਗਨ ਮੈ ਥਾਲੁ; ਰਵਿ ਚੰਦ ਦੀਪਕ ਬਨੇ;ਤਾਰਕਾ ਮੰਡਲਾ ਜਨਕ ਮੋਤੀ।

ਧੂਪ ਮਲਿਆਨ ਲੋ; ਪਵਨ ਚਵਰੇ ਕਰੇ;ਸਗਲਬਨਰਾਇ ਫੂਲੰਤ ਜੋਤੀ।

ਕੈਸੀ ਆਰਤੀ ਹੋਇ, ਭਵ ਖੰਡਨਾ! ਤੇਰੀ ਆਰਤੀ।

ਅਨਹਤਾ ਸ਼ਬਦ ਵਾਜੰਤ ਭੇਰੀ।

ਸਹੱਸ ਤਵ ਨੇਨ, ਨਨ ਨੈਨ ਹੈ ਤੋਹਿ ਕੋ;ਸਹੱਸ ਮੂਰਤ, ਨਨਾ ਏਕ ਤੋਹੀ;

ਸਹੱਸ ਪਦ ਬਿਮਲ, ਨਨ ਏਕ ਪਦ;ਗੰਧ ਬਿਨ, ਸਹੱਸ ਤਵ ਗੰਧ; ਇਵ ਚਲਤ ਮੋਹੀ।

ਸਭ ਮੈ ਜੋਤ ਜੋਤ ਹੈ ਸੋਇ,

ਤਿਸਕੇ ਚਾਨਨ ਸਭ ਮਹਿ ਚਾਨਨੁ ਹੋਇ।

ਗੁਰ ਸਾਖੀ ਜੋਤ ਪ੍ਰਗਟ ਹੋਇ।

ਜੋ ਤਿਸ ਭਾਵੈ ਸੋ ਆਰਤੀ ਹੋਇ।

ਹਰਿ ਚਰਨ ਕਮਲ ਮੁਕਰੰਦ ਲੋਭਤ, ਮਨੁ ਅਨਦਿਨੋ ਮੋਹਿ ਆਹੀ ਪਿਆਸਾ।

ਕਿਰਪਾ ਜਲਦੇ ਨਾਨਕ ਸਾਰੰਗ ਕਉ। ਹੋਇ ਜਾਂਤੇ ਤੇਰੇ ਨਾਇ ਵਾਸਾ।।

being. "In His Court," said Guru Nanak, "there are lacs of Muhammads, lacs of Brahmas, of Vishnus and of Maheshas (Shivas), lacs of Ramas the great, and lacs of others, in lacs of garbs."[55] On this the Sultan got enraged and ordered him to be imprisoned. When he was being driven out of the Darbar Hall to be led to the Jail, he addressed the Sultan as follows:--

> Beautiful features and clothes wilt thou leave behind,
> Thy own good and bad deeds will go with thee!
> Order here as thou wilt, narrow is the way by which thou
> shalt have to go,
>
> When thou shall be taken naked to the hell,
> verily, thou shalt look horribly ugly;
> Thou wilt then repent for thy bad deeds.[56]

Thus was Guru Nanak imprisoned in the Delhi Jail, in the year 1526, of Christ. Ah! cruel and ungreatful humanity, well dost thou treat, repay and reward thy reformers for all their trouble to elevate thee! But wherever God's *prophets* may be, they do not fail to make the best of their time and to perform their mission, even in the adverse circumstances. Guru Nanak is said to have passed his time in Jail in trying to reform the thieves, robbers, murderers and other criminals among whom he was lodged. He pitied the degraded conditions of the inmates

---

55 *Bhai* Banno's copy of *Granth* sahid, Shlo M, 1 at the end of the volume. This copy has not yet been printed.

ਜਿਤ ਦਰ ਲਖ ਮੁਹੱਮਦਾ ਲਖ ਬ੍ਰਹਮੇ ਬਿਸ਼ਨ ਮਹੇਸ,
ਲਖ ਲਖ ਰਾਮ ਵਡੀਰੀਏ, ਲਖ ਰਾਹੀ ਲਖ ਵੇਸ।

56 Asa Di Var, M. 1 Pauri 14.

ਕਪੜ ਰੂਪ ਸੁਹਾਵਣਾ ਛਡਿ ਦੁਨੀਆਂ ਅੰਦਰਿ ਜਾਵਣਾ,
ਚੰਗਾ ਮੰਦਾ ਆਪਣਾ ਆਪੇ ਹੀ ਕੀਤਾ ਪਾਵਣਾ,
ਹੁਕਮ ਕੀਏ ਮਨ ਭਾਂਵਦੇ ਰਾਹਿ ਭੀੜੇ ਅਗੇ ਜਾਵਣਾ;
ਨੰਗਾ ਦੋਜਖਿ ਚਾਲਿਆਂ ਤਾਂ ਦਿਸੇ ਖਰਾ ਡਰਾਵਣਾ।
ਕਰ ਅਉਗਣ ਪਛੋਤਾਵਣਾ।

of that dungeon and sympathised with them from the bottom of his heart. He began to teach and reform them. And it is also said that the labour that he had to do for his bread within the Jail precincts, simple imprisonment being quite unknown during those days, used to be done by itself. It seems probable that his part of the labour was performed by other prisoners, to whom he has endeared himself by his friendly and noble advice. It was perhaps predestined that, having proclaimed his doctrine to the world at large, he was also to raise the criminals in Jail from their pitiful and reckless condition, because their misdeed had placed them under physical restraint and because, on account of their loss of liberty, they could not attend and hear his sermons, which were delivered to the general populace.

10 Release

Whatever the advantages of Guru Nanak's incarceration may have been to the suffering humanity, it should not be forgotten that Guru Nanak was sent into imprisonment under circumstances which totally unjustify the procedure adopted by the Lodhi despot. The glaring piece of injustice done to him brought with its natural consequences. Such flagrant and manifest misdeeds do but bring about revolutions. These are but the sacrifices which humanity requires for her regeneration. The sacrifices of Guru Nanak's personal liberty served, as it were, to bring about a change in the Government of the country within few months. The ministers of Sultan Ibrahim invited *Babar*, who already in possession of the western Punjab, to come over and take possession of the Delhi throne. *Baba*r was the last person to lose such a golden opportunity. Only a single contest on the memorable field of Panipat decided the fate of the Afghan Rule in India, and *Baba*r was proclaimed Emperor of Delhi. In his visit of inspection of the prisons, Babar, about whose advent Guru Nanak had already predicted, in the course of his talk with *Bhai* Lalo at Amenabad, a few years before, singled out the Guru from among the prisoners, and took him to the Durbar, where after a brief but instructive conversation he was honourably released.

Before Guru Nanak's departure, *Baba*r asked him to accept the Muhammadan faith which recognized only one God as he himself did. In Islam, he said, he could have the additional advantage of a recommendation for salvation by God's holy and last prophet, Muhammad. To this Guru Nanak replied as follows:–

> There is but One God
> > True and Unknowable;
> And millions of Muhammads are waiting at
> > His court and cannot be numbered.

> Prophet sent come into this world
> (But) whenever He so likes, they are sent for,
> bound hand and foot.
> This I, Nanak, His salve, have ascertained,
> > That God alone is hole, all other are profane.[57]

Babar, instead of taking offence at this, showed greatest courtesy and kindness to Guru Nanak and requested him to accept some present for him. But Guru Nanak refused to do so, saying,

> "I am gifted by one God,
> > Whose gifts everyone enjoys.

---

57 *Bhai* Bala's *Janamsakhi.*
ਲਖ ਮੁਹੱਮਦ, ਏਕ ਖੁਦਾਇ।
ਅਲਖ ਸੱਚਾ ਹੈ ਬੇ ਪਰਵਾਹਿ।
ਕਈ ਮੁਹੱਮਦ ਖੜੇ ਦਰਬਾਰ।
ਸ਼ੁਮਾਰ ਨ ਪਾਵੈਂ ਬੇਸ਼ੁਮਾਰ।
ਰਸੂਲ ਰਸਾਲ ਦੁਨੀਆਂ ਮੇਂ ਆਇਆ।
ਜਬ ਚਾਹਿਆ ਤਬ ਪਕੜ ਮੰਗਾਇਆ।
ਇਉ ਸਹੀ ਕੀਆ ਹੈ ਨਾਨਕ ਬੰਦੇ।
ਪਾਕ ਖੁਦਾਇ ਅਉਰ ਸਭ ਗੰਦੇ।

He who looks to human support,
Loses the world as well as his faith.

There is only one Giver, and the whole world is a beggar,
He who looks to others than Him for support Loses all
his honor and respect.
Kings and emperors are all made by Him,
And no one is His equal,

Hear O, *Babar Meer*, what Nanak says,
Foolish is the *faqeer* who begs of thee.[58]

After this the genial and illustrious monarch gladly permitted
Guru Nanak to depart.

11 Hardwar (Second visit)

From Kartarpore Guru Nanak started to north, travelled
to Kashmere and paying visits to several other hill-stations,
reached Hardwar on the occasion of the great *Kumbhi mela*.
People from all parts of India had flocked to the banks of the
holy river to have a plunge in the sacred water. Nanak was
no doubt now somewhat old and weak in body, but he could
not throw away his opportunity of preaching his gospel to the
assembled multitude. After washing their sins in the Ganges,

---

58 *Bhai* Bala's *Janamsakhi*
ਈਮਾ ਦੀਆ ਏਕ ਖੁਦਾਇ।
ਜਿਸ ਕਾ ਦੀਆ ਸਭ ਕੋਈ ਖਾਇ।
ਬੰਦੇ ਦੀ ਜੋ ਲੇਵੇ ਉਟ।
ਦੀਨ ਦੁਨੀਆਂ ਹੈ ਤਿਸਕਾਉ ਤੋਟ।
ਇਕ ਦਾਤਾ ਸਭ ਜਗਤ ਭਿਖਾਰੀ।
ਤਿਸਕੋ ਛਾਡ ਅਵਰ ਕੋ ਲਾਗੇ ਉਨ ਸਗਲੀ ਪਤ ਹਾਰੀ।
ਸ਼ਾਹ ਸੁਲਤਾਨ ਸਭ ਤਿਸ ਕੇ ਕੀਏ।
ਉਸ ਕੇ ਸਾਥ ਨ ਕੋਇ ਰਲਈਏ।
ਕਹੇ ਨਾਨਕ ਸੁਨ ਬਾਬਰ ਮੀਰ।
ਤੁਝ ਤੇ ਮਾਂਗੇ ਸੁ ਐਹਮਕ ਫਕੀਰ।

the people, with their faces turned to the east, were offering handfuls of the holy water to the sun and their own ancestors. Guru Nanak saw his opportunity, at once entered the river, and, with his face to west, began to throw bushels of water out of the river. A large crowd of astonished people gathered around him and enquired what he was doing. "I am watering my fields at Kartarpore; they are getting parched by the scorching heat of the sun, for want of rains." Where be thy fields and thy Kartarpore?" asked a voice. "They are on the Ravi in the Punjab," said Guru Nanak. On this they burst forth into laugher and said, "How can thy fields be watered from such a long distance? Fool shouldst thou be to do so." "And bigger fools are you, my friends. If this water in such a large quantity cannot reach my fields on this very earth, some three or four hundred miles away, how can a handful of it satiate your ancestors and the sun, so far off, you don't know where? Leave off these idle pursuits and worship God who creates, feeds and waters all. Useless are these ceremonies and formalities. The Ganges water cannot wash away your sins, but that may be done by *Bhakti* and Devotion. Change your hearts, perform good deeds, and be saved." Needless to add that these words acted like magic in people's mind and all got silenced. The commandment contained in them vibrated in many hearts and Guru Nanak added good many more converts in the number of his followers, then and there.

౦౩౭౦

CHAPTER 8
LAST DAYS AND DEATH

Guru Nanak's mission had made a fair progress about the year 1530. He had proclaimed his princtiples and doctrines loudly in all parts of southern Asia, from Arabia and (probably) Turkey in the west to Burma in the east, and from Kashmere in the north to Ceylon in the South. No less than 30 *Manjis* scattered over all these vast countries, seem to have been established by him to continue the work of local preaching, and now he had established a center at Kartarpore where the Sikhs could gather occasionally and where they could focus their affections and devotion. Representatives of nearly all the religious denominations, sects as well as ascetic orders, had severally their share of notice by him, and it was now high time for the establishment of some bond of union between his followers. This bond was provided by the "Guru at Kartarpore." From his last trip to the Kashmere, Himalayas and Hardwar Guru Nanak returned to Kartarpore in about 1531 and remained there for the rest of his life.

The future careers of at least two men, out of those whom Guru Nanak converted at Kartarpore, entitle them to a special mention here. The one was Bura of a small village, called Ramdas, about 3 miles distant from Kartarpore. Though young in years, Bura was a man of great wisdom, unflinching faith and earnest devotion to the cause of Sikhism, and so far back as the very moment of his conversion to the Sikh faith he was held to be one of the wisest heads present at Kartarpore. The brief story of his conversion to the Church of Guru Nanak runs thus:-

Bhai Budha's Conversion

One day Bura came to Guru Nanak and prostrated himself before him and said, "O Guru ji, a few days back the powerful Afghans forcibly cut and took away all our crops, ripe and unripe, and we were all helpless against them.It was *then* that it struck me that if we could not save ourselves from these Afghans, how shall we possibly be able to get saved from the all-powerful hands of Death. I have heard of thee a good deal and have full faith in thee. Pray, do tell me the way of salvation on the day of great danger and horror." Thus said Bura; to which Guru Nanak replied, as follows:- "It is God alone who can be the support of all on the day of Judgement. If thou wantest to be saved, O Bura, Serve God So That God May Save Thee!" These words were sufficient to convert the innocent and sincere heart of Bura, and from that moment ever afterwards, Bura was known as one of the chief missionaries of Guru Nanak's Church, present at Kartarpore. His wise talk entitled him to a place in assemblies of old experienced persons, and he therefore won the title of *Bhai* Budha (The oldman). He made himself so much useful that Guru Nanak, at the time of his ascension, richly rewarded him for his sincerity of devotion and purity of faith. He was entrusted with the performance of the sacred ceremony of installing the successive Gurus, and had the honour of seating no less than five Gurus on the chief *Manji* with his own hands.

The second was still a greater man. Lehna, for this was his name, hailed from a small village in Ferozpore District, and was a zealous idol-worshipper before his conversion. He used to visit the temple of the goddess Vaishnav Devi, in the Kashmere hills, every year and was followed every time by a large number of his neighborus and relatives. He was the leader of the party, who used to travel stage by stage to the hill mansion of the goddess. Shortly after Guru Nanak settled at Kartarpore, Lehna was going on one of his usual annual visits, at the head of his party, to Vaishnav Devi, when they chanced to halt at a place not very distant from Kartarpore. Somebody told him of the presence of Guru Nanak at Kartarpore, and he thought it worthwhile to pay a short visit, by the way, to the much praised saint. He came to the Guru and was very much pleased to see and talk with him. He was already of a religious bent of mind, and no great effort on the part of Guru Nanak was needed to convert him to his own faith. Guru Nanak's natural and holy talk convinced him that he had wasted all his past years in vain pursuits, and the place where his soul could get entire satisfaction had after all been suddenly thrown open to him. "What is your name? O man," asked Nanak. "My Name is Lehna, Guruji," said he. "Thy *lehna*[59] is here then, where else art thou going for it?" Lehna remained with the Guru and refused to go any further. Legend says that early in the morning on the day after his arrival he saw the goddess Vaishnav Devi, whose image he had been seeing at the place of his past pilgrimages, sweeping the floor of the Guru's abode with a brush, and that on questioning her she told him that she was only an humble one of the maids at the door of the Guru. We may believe this legend or not, *Bhai* Lehna's sudden and complete conversion, and his extreme devotion to the Guru's cause thereafter, are matters of no small moment. His unflinching faith was put to many a hard test; and it was not till after he had succeeded in placing the purity of his faith and morals and the extreme obedience and devotion to the Guru and his cause, beyond even the distant possibility of a doubt, that he was fixed upon by Guru Nanak as his successor.

---

59 Lehna in Punjabi means the article which is due to one from another ; which another owes to him; which one has to receive from another.

For about eight years, Guru Nanak presided, at Kartarpore, over the deliberations of the Sikhs, and guided their movements and conduct with his own hands. But his end was now approaching nigh. In September, 1539, he asked *Bhai* Budha to instal *Bhai* Lehna on the Chief *Manji* which he himself at once abandoned. *Bhai* Budha performed the sacred function, as desired. Guru Nanak then placed some presents before *Bhai* Lehna and bowed down to him. On getting up, he hailed *Bhai* Lehna as Angad Guru (Guru made of his own self). Thus it is said that, the spirit of Guru Nanak quietly passed on to *Bhai* Lehna, who was at once acknowledged by the Sikh brotherhood as embodiment thereof. All the Sikhs then bowed down before Guru Angad, as directed by Guru Nanak, and the latter passed on to everlasting arms of the Almighty Father, two days after this event.

Guru Nanak's cosmopolitan views were equally acceptable to the Hindus and Muhammadans, though the more orthodox and staunch of both of them sometimes took offence at his outspoken utterances, and just as Hindus had ultimately, though gradually, followed him, so had also men of Mussalman origin attached themselves to his doctrines. It may however here be pointed out that these two sections of his followers were yet quite distinct in their social habits and customs. Now that the Guru's body was no more living among them, these two sections quarreled against each other on the question whether the body was to be cremated or buried. The struggle was raging furiously when lo, the discovery was made and announced that the body of the Guru had disappeared from under the white sheet of cloth which covered him while he was dying! This put an end to all discussion, and the wise counsel of *Bhai* Budha prevailed, acording to which one half of the covering was given to Mussalman followers to bury and the other half to Hindus to burn. This both of them did, and thus ended the days upon this rugged earth of one of the noblest sons of God.

In the conclusion, it may also be noted that before his ascension, a few of the Hindu followers had taken an opportunity to ask Guru Nanak if all the death ceremonies of the Hindus[60] had to be performed after him. In reply to this question, Guru Nanak had addressed them his last precept as follows:-

Let remembrance of the One Name be the 'lamp,'
    in which is consumed all pain for oil;
That giveth light and this soaketh up, and thus is
    the meeting with *Yama* avoided.

O people! Do not perform hypocritical deeds.
    Lacs of reels of cotton are consumed by a grain of fire(or
lacs of hypocrisies cannot approach a grain of love.)

My *Pind* and *Pattal* is God Himself, and the funeral obsequies
    only the remembrance of the True Name of the Creator.

Here and there, in future as in the past, He alone is my support.

Singing God's praise is as the Ganges (Hardwar) and Benares,
    wherein the spirit bathes:
    His is the true bathing who day and night entertains
Love for God.

Heavenly and earthly oblations are all made and eaten
    up by a Brahman;

---

60 Hindus light a lamp after a man's death and think that it lights the path of the deceased through the infernal regions. They also offer Pind and Pattal, a kind of oblation and food in the name of the deceased to the Brahamans through whom they hope the deceased to get satisfied of his hunger, &c. during his voyage through those regions. These oblations are of two sorts; One called heavenly and the other earthly. They also throw the bones of the deceased in the Ganges at Hardwar and themselves bathe in the sacred river there as well as at Benares in the hope of benefitting the soul of the deceased.

It is the oblation of the Grace of God which can never be spent up, says Nanak.[61]

ॐ

---

61 Rag Asa, M. 1 Gh 3, Sh 32.
ਦੀਵਾ ਮੇਰਾ ਏਕੁ ਨਾਮੁ, ਦੁਖੁ ਵਿਚਿ ਪਾਇਆ ਤੇਲੁ।
ਉਨਿ ਚਾਨਣਿ, ਇਨਿ ਸੋਖਿਆ, ਚੁਕਾ ਜਮ ਸਿਉ ਮੇਲੁ।
ਲੋਕਾ, ਮਤ ਕੋ ਫਕੜੁ ਪਾਇ।
ਲਖੁ ਮੜਿਆ ਕਰਿ ਏਕਠੇ, ਏਕ ਰਤੀਲੇ ਭਾਇ।
ਪਿੰਡੁ ਪਤਲੁ ਮੇਰੀ ਕੇਸਉ, ਕਿਰਿਆ ਸਚੁ ਨਾਮੁ ਕਰਤਾਰੁ।
ਏਥੈ, ਉਥੈ, ਆਗੈ ਪਾਛੈ, ਇਹੁ ਮੇਰਾ ਆਧਾਰੁ।
ਗੰਗੁ ਬਨਾਰਸਿ ਸਿਫਤਿ ਤੁਮਾਰੀ ਨਾਂਵੈ ਆਤਮ ਰਾਉ।
ਸਾਚਾ ਨਾਵਣੁ ਤਾ ਥੀਐ ਜਾਂ ਇਹ ਨਿਸ ਲਾਗੈ ਭਾਉ।
ਇਕ ਲੋਕੀ, ਹੋਰ ਛਮਛਰੀ, ਬ੍ਰਾਹਮਣ ਵਟ ਪਿੰਡ ਖਾਇ।
ਨਾਨਕ ਪਿੰਡ ਬਖਸੀਸ ਕਾ, ਕਬਹੂ ਨਿਖੂਟਸ ਨਾਇ।।

CHAPTER 9
THE CREED OF GURU NANAK

Were the men who comprehended God best deist or pantheists? Ranan, in his *Life of Christ*, holds this question to be meaningless. Physical and metaphysical proofs of the existence of God, he says, would have been quite indifferent of these great men. They felt the divine within themselves. The paltry discussions about deism and pantheism have stifled all fertile ideas of the divine in the breast of modern rationalism. In trying to comprehend and explain the incomprehensible problem of Existence man does but suspend for the time his emotional and divine sentiments, which after a time, cease to respond to any tender calls. His mental labours prove fruitless and he gets bewildered.

Nanak was not a speculative philosopher. In him we find nothing resembling the imagination and the hallucination of a Shankracharya. He never gave utterance to the sacrilegious idea that he was God. He had no visions. He dwelt in the bosom of God by direct and constant communion with Him. He believed himself to be the servant of God. God was in him and he felt himself with God. From his heart he drew all that he taught of his Father. God conceived as Father or Husband – such was the theology of Nanak. And this was not with him a theoretical principle, a doctrine more or less proved, which he sought to inculcate in others. He did not argue with his disciples; he exacted from them no effort of attention. His are the outpourings of a sincere, true, tender, sympathetic and devoted heart, filled with unbounded love for God.

Guru Nanak did not formulate any elaborate system of philosophy. In fact he did not care to discover how the universe was created, or which things in this universe were eternal and which transitory. He took the world as he found it, and began to teach and reform. He taught people as to what they ought to be, not so much as to what they have been or whence they have come and whither they had to go.

He loved humanity and wanted to save her. "There is much in the character and teaching of Nanak," says Sir Lepel Griffin, "which reminds the student of the life and teaching of the great Buddhist reformer, whose devotion to the cause of humanity and the general enlightenment of whose doctrine have had so vast an influence upon a quarter of the human race."[62] To use the words of Mr. Muhammad Latif,[63] Guru Nanak's best endeavours during his long public career were directed towards removing, or reducing to a minimum, those religious and social differences which had sprung up between the two great religious sects of India, the Hindus and the Muhammadans, and to reconciling them both, and to a great extent he was successful. He viewed with disfavour the intolerance of the Mussalmans towards the Hindus, and the percepts of his religion inculcated peace to all mankind, brotherly love to one another, and living virtuously and harmoniously. "He set himself to teach men the way of salvation, not as a ruler, but as a servant to God, to whom the light had been shown, coming to bring, not strife among men, but peace.[64]

His essential character was that of a reformer in the best and truest sense of the word, and his religion is one possessing

---

62 *Ranjit Singh, * Rulers of India ' Series.
63 *History of the Punjab.*
64 Sir C. Gough's *The Sikh and the Sikh wars*

a noble ideal, practical and social meaning. His great object was to raise Hinduism and Islam alike from the lowest depths of polytheism and superstition, of conventions and formalities, into which they had fallen, and to preach in addition a nobler doctrine, a purer morality and a more exclusive monotheism.

The religious sect, founded by Guru Nanak is based on two fundamental principles; the Unity of God and the Brotherhood of Man. "A seeker after truth from his earliest years, he tried study, solitary meditation, travel and intercourse with his neighbours," says Sir C. Gough, "but failed to find either in Islam or in the current Hinduism the satisfaction which his soul desired, but he penetrated beneath the crust of observances and conventions, and found the root of the matter in the Unity of God and the equality of men before Him."[65]

"There is but One God, whose name is True, the Creator, the All-pervading, devoid of fear and enmity, Immortal, Unborn, Self-begotten, the Great and the Gracious. Him I worship. He was True in the beginning, He was True in the primal age, He is True now, and He will ever be True, says Nanak."[66] "Why worship the second, who takes birth and dies; worship the One alone who pervades the lands and the waters." [67] "Whom shall I call the second? There is none. In all there is that Spotless One.[68] Numerous Muhammads have there been,

---

65 *The Sikhs and the Sikh wars.*

66 Japji Sahib, *Pauri* 1.

ੴ, ਸੱਤ ਨਾਮ, ਕਰਤਾ, ਪੁਰਖ,
ਨਿਰਭਉ, ਨਿਰਵੈਰ, ਅਕਾਲ ਮੁਰਤ, ਅਜੂਨੀ, ਸੈਭੰ,
ਗੁਰ, ਪ੍ਰਸਾਦ। ਜਪਿ ਆਦਿ ਸਚੁ, ਜੁਗਾਦਿ ਸੱਚੁ, ਹੈਭੀ
ਸਚੁ, ਨਾਨਕੁ, ਹੋਸੀ ਭੀ ਸਚੁ॥

67 *Shlok* M. 1.

ਦੂਜਾ ਕਾਹੇ ਸਿਮਰੀਐ, ਜਮੇ ਤੇ ਮਰ ਜਾਇ,
ਏਕੋ ਸਿਮਰੋ ਨਾਨਕ, ਜੋ ਜਲ ਥਲ ਰਹਿਆ ਸਮਾਇ।

68 Rag Gowree, M. 1, Aslit, Go – araree, *Shlok* 5 (Rahao)

ਦੂਜ ਕਉਨ ਕਹਾਂ? ਨਹੀਂ ਕੋਈ॥
ਸਭ ਮੈ ਏਕ ਨਿਰੰਜਨ ਸੋਈ॥

and multitudes of Brahmas, Vishnoos and Shivas, thousands of *peers* and *prophets*, and lacs of saints and holy men: "But the Chief of Lords is the One Lord, Creator, God of the True Name. O Nanak! His qualities, without and beyond reckoning, are beyond comprehension."[69] Do not fall in useless struggles, worship not another than God, bow not to the Dead."[70]

Nanak combined the excellencies of preceding reformers, says Cunningham, in his *History of the Sikhs* and he avoided the more grave errors into which they had fallen. Instead of the circumscribed divinity, the anthropomorphous God of Ramanand and Kabir he loftily invokes the Lord as the one, the sole, the timeless being, the creator, self-existent, the incomprehensible and the everlasting. He likens the Deity to truth, which was before the world began, which is, and which shall endure for ever, as the ultimate idea or cause of all we know and behold. He addresses equally the *Mullah* and *Pundit*, the *Dervaish* and the *Sannyasee* and he tells them to remember that Lord of Lords who had been come and go numberless Muhammads, Vishnus and Shivas.

"For Nanak," says Frederic Pincot, in his essay on 'Sikhism' in *The Religious Systems of the World*, "there was no such thing as a God for Hindus, a god for the Muhammadans, and a god or gods for the outer heathen; for him there was but one God, not in the likeness of man, like Rama; not a creature of attributes and passions, like the Allah of Muhammad; but one, sole, indivisible, self-existent, incomprehensible, timeless, all-pervading, - to be named, but otherwise indescribable and altogether lovely. Such was Nanak's idea of the Creator and Sustainer of the phenomenal world, and it was a conception

---

69 *Bhai* Banno's Manuscript copy of *Granth Sahib Shlok* M. 1 at the end of the Volume.

ਸਿਰ ਨਾਥਾਂ ਕੇ ਏਕ ਨਾਥਿ ਸਤਿਨਾਮ ਕਰਤਾਰ।
ਨਾਨਕ ਤਾਂਕੀ ਕੀਮਤ ਨਾ ਪਵੈ ਬੇਅੰਤ ਬੇਸ਼ੁਮਾਰ।

70 Rag Sorath, M. 1, Asth, Sh. 1(1).

ਦੁਬਿਧਾ ਨ ਪੜਹੁ, ਹਰਿ ਬੀਨੁ ਹੋਰੁ ਨ ਪੂਜਊ, ਮੜੇ ਮਸਾਣਿ ਨ ਜਾਈ।

which at once abrogated all petty distinctions of creed, sect, dogma, and ceremony. The realisation of such a God shatters the sophistries of the theologian and the quibblings of the dialecticians, it clears the brow from the gloom of abstruse pondering over trifles and leaves the heart free for the exercise of human sympathies."

The great philosophers of the world have tried their utmost to comprehend and describe God's nature, and have consequently been lost in the total obscurity of the subject matter of their labours. Even the great Buddha himself spent many of his useful years in the vain pursuit of comprehending God, but he too was so much baffled that he had to take shelter ultimately in the doctrine of total nothingness. To him all that we see and behold appeared to have evolved out of nothing, and into nothing they had to relapse. There was no God, no soul and no matter, which could be called eternal, and the highest object of man was to become extinct, to get totally annihilated, to attain *Nirvan*, as he called it. On the other hand, the great *Rishis* of old have also expressed quite contradictory views about the existence and nature of God, so that the student gets quite bewildered in the huge mass of controversy that raged about this point. But in the creed of Guru Nanak, God has been described so as to admit of no contradiction. It is His nature to be beyond comprehension and beyond description. That which is comprehended and which can be explained and defined *is not God.* "Invisible, Indefinite, Incomprehensible, Unperceivable, Timeless, without destiny, without caste, without birth, self-existent, without attachments and without apprehensions!"[71] God characterised thus is the Deity worshipped by Guru Nanak. 'He is neither established, nor created. He Himself is the Pure One. They who have served him have obtained honour. Sing of Him, the Sum-total of all virtues," says Nanak, "Sing, hear and put

---

71 Rag Sorath, M. 1, Sh 6(1.)

ਅਲਖ, ਅਪਾਰ, ਅਗਮ, ਅਗੋਚਰਿ, ਨਾ ਤਿਸੁ ਕਾਲੁ, ਨ ਕਰਮਾ,
ਜਾਤਿ ਅਜਾਤਿ, ਅਜੋਨੀ, ਸੰਭਉ, ਨਾਤਿਸੁ ਭਾਉ, ਨ ਭਰਮਾ

His love unto your hearts. Thus shall your sorrows be removed and beatitude attained".[72] God is ever true, He is the True Lord, and of True Name. He who made the Universe, is and will be. He will neither depart, nor made to depart. He alone, who with his hands created all things of different colours, descriptions and species, beholds his handi work, which attests of his greatness. He will do what pleaseth Himself ; no order may be issued to Him. He is the King, the King of Kings, and all remain subject to His will, says Nanak."[73] Thus the Deity, under whatever name known, as Brahm, Hari, Ram, Govind, Allah, &c., is incomprehensible, invisible, uncreated, eternal, and alone possessing any real existence. "Brahma, reported to have been born of the lotus-leaf that appeared out of the navel of Vishnu, recited the *Vedas* with a clear mouth and throat; but he too could not comprehend His greatness and metempsychosis remained under mist."[74]

---

72 Japji Sahib *Pauri* 5.

ਥਾਪਿਆ ਨ ਜਾਇ, ਕੀਤਾ ਨ ਹੋਇ।
ਆਪੇ ਆਪ ਨਿਰੰਜਨ ਸੋਇ।
ਜਿਨ ਸੇਵਿਆ ਤਿਨ ਪਾਇਆ ਮਾਨ।
ਨਾਨਕ ਗਾਵੀਐ ਗੁਣੀ ਨਿਧਾਨ।
ਗਾਵੀਐ ਸੁਣਿਐ, ਮਨ ਰਖੀਐ ਭਾਉ।
ਦੁੱਖ ਪਰ ਹਰ ਸੁਖ ਘਰ ਲੈ ਜਾਉ।

73 Japji Sahib *Pauri* 27

ਸੋਈ ਸੋਈ ਸਦਾ ਸਚ ਸਾਹਿਬ ਸਾਚਾ ਸਾਚੀ ਨਾਈ।
ਹੈ ਭੀ, ਹੋਸੀ, ਜਾਇ, ਨ ਜਾਸੀ, ਰਚਨਾ ਜਿਨ ਰਚਾਈ।
ਰੰਗੀ ਰੰਗੀ ਭਾਂਤੀ ਕਰ ਕਰ ਜਿਨ ਸੀ ਮਾਇਆ ਜਿਨ ਉਪਾਈ।
ਕਰ ਕਰ ਵੇਖੇ ਕੀਤਾ ਆਪਣਾ, ਜਿਊ ਤਿਸਦੀ ਵਡਿਆਈ।
ਜੋ ਤਿਸ ਭਾਵੇ ਸੋਈ ਕਰਸੀ, ਫਿਰ ਹੁਕਮ ਨ ਕਰਨਾ ਜਾਈ।
ਸੋ ਪਾਤਸ਼ਾਹਾਂ, ਸ਼ਾਹ ਪਾਤਸ਼ਾਹਿਬੁ, ਨਾਨਕ ਰੈਹਨ ਰਜਾਈ।

74 Rag Goojri M.1, Gh. 1 Sh 2(1.)

ਨਾਭਿ ਕਮਲ ਤੇ ਬ੍ਰਹਮਾ ਉਪਜੇ, ਵੇਦ ਪੜਹਿ ਮੁਖੀ ਕੰਠ ਸਵਾਰਿ;
ਤਾਂਕੋ ਅੰਤੁ ਨ ਜਾਈ ਲਖਣਾ ਆਵਤ ਜਾਤ ਰਹੈਗੁ ਬਾਰੀ।

Nanak adopted, says Cunningham,[75] the philosophical systems of his countrymen and regarded bliss as the dwelling of the soul with God. He makes the constant use of the current language or notions of the time on good many other subjects, and says that 'he who remains bright and amid darkness, unmoved, amid deception, that is, perfect amid temptations, should attain happiness.' Guru Nanak also referred to the Arabian prophet, and to the Hindu Incarnation, not as impostors and the diffusers of evil, but as having been truly sent by God to instruct mankind, and he lamented that sin should nevertheless prevail. Such references to the Hindu incarnations and to the Hindu philosophy have led many a writer to hold that Nanak implicitly believed them as objects of worship and faith. Dr. Ernest Trump openly commits himself to this mistaken notion and says, "We should be wrong in assuming that Nanak forbade the worship of other gods on the ground of the unity of the Supreme. Far from doing so, he took over the whole Hindu Pantheon, with all its mythological background, with the only difference that the whole was subordinated to the Supreme Brahm. The position of the popular gods was, thereby, though not openly attacked, naturally lowered and their service must needs appear less important, yea even useless for the attainment of the highest object of mankind." A little further on, Dr. Trump remarks that ' it is a mistake if Nanak is represented as having endeavoured to unite the Hindu and Muhammadan idea about God. Nanak remained a thorough Hindu according to all his views, and if he had communionship with Mussalmans and many of these even became his disciples, it was owing to the fact that Sufism which all these Muhamadans were professing, was in reality nothing but a Pantheism, derived directly from Hindu sources, and only outwardly adapted to the forms of the Islam.[76] The whole of this lengthy discussion of the German Translator of a portion of *Adi Granth* is based on the notion that a regular

---

75 *History of the Sikhs.*
76 Translation of the *Adi Granth.*

system of philosophy can be evolved out of the *Granth Sahib*, while strange as it may appear, he himself somewhat rightly observes that "Guru Nanak was not a speculative philosopher." All his criticism of what appears to him defective in the train of philosophical thought, as he has tried to gather out of the *Granth*, is quite a labour lost, and he ought to have remembered that if Guru Nanak employed the Hinduised language in his teachings, this does not justify the charge laid against him of believing in the Hindu Pantheon.

Professor Wilson[77] also would, with Dr. Trump, appear to think slightingly of the doctrines of Nanak, as being mere metaphysical notions founded on the abstractions of Soofeeism and the Vedant philosophy. "But, it is difficult," says Cunningham, "for any one to write about the omnipotence of God and the hopes of man, without laying himself open to the charge of belonging to one speculative school or another." Captain Cunningham quotes certain epigrams and sayings of St. Paul and others, and says that "such expressions as, 'Doth not the Lord fill heaven and earth', 'God in whom we live and move and have our being,' and 'of Him, and to Him, and through Him are all things,' might be used to declare the Prophet and the Apostle to the Pantheists or Materialists? But it nevertheless seems plain that Jeremiah and Paul, and likewise Nanak, had another object in view than scholastic dogmatism, and that they simply desired to impress mankind with exalted notions of the greatness and goodness of God by a vague employment of general language which they knew would never mislead the multitude."

"It is to be remembered," says Hallam,[78] "that the Sikhs regard the mission of Nanak and Govind as the consummation of other dispensations including that of Mahomet, and their talk, therefore, of Brahma and Vishnu, and various heavenly powers,

---

77 As Res XVII 233 and continuation of Mills *History of India* VII pp 101, 102 ; quoted in Cunningham's *History of the Sikhs.*
78 Middle ages iii 346 quoted in Cunningham's *History of the Sikhs.*

　　　　　　THE CREED OF GURU NANAK

is no more unreasonable than the deference of Christians to Moses and Abraham, and to the arch-angles Michael and Gabriel. Such allusions are perhaps more excusable in the Sikhs, than the 'singular polytheism of Christian medieval divines, which they grafted on the language, rather (indeed) the principles of Christianity."

"Nanak, indeed, refers continually to Hindu notions, but he was not therefore an idolater," says Cunningham, "and it should further be borne in mind that as St. John could draw illustrations from Greak philosophy, so could St. Paul make an advantageous use of the Greek poets, as was long ago observed upon, in a right spirit by Milton (Speech for the Liberty of Unlicensed Printing). In the early ages of Christianity, moreover, the sybiline leaves were referred to as foretelling the mission of Jesus, but although the spuriousness of the passages is now admitted, the Fathers are not accused of Polytheism, or of holding Amalthen, a nurse of Jupiter, to be a real type of the Virgin Mary."

It would thus appear that if Guru Nanak has sometimes drawn illustrations from the Hindu sources, it does not follow from it that he himself cherished the exact ideas, contained in those illustrations, as objects of his faith. For let it be remembered that he has likewise drawn upon the Muhammadan sources for his sermons. For this purpose the reader may only be referred back to Guru Nanak's sermon in the Musjid at Sultanpore, where he does not denounce Islam, but has only tried to express a better and holier view thereof. Guru Nanak's use of the popular language should not therefore be mistaken for his faith which later can only be ascertained by viewing Guru Nanak's work as a whole and interpreting his utterances more liberally.

The next fundamental principle of Guru Nanak's religion is the Brotherhood of Man without distinction of race, caste or creed. He did not recognise the distinction of caste, which is the fundamental institution, resting on religious sanction, of Hinduism. "Caste may be generally described as the theory and practice of heredity social distinctions carried to the extremest limits and confirmed by the sanction of religion. The spirit is more or less present in most societies which have attained a high organisation. But carried to an extreme it is a barrier to all progress, since it is in effect an enormous system of privilege."*[79] Guru Nanak knew for certain that religious reform and social progress were impossible without breaking through the shackles of caste. So long as the idea of a higher and nobler birth prevailed, with an exclusive sway over people's minds, no sort of progress could be possible, and the supposed righteousness of the Pharisee could not let him mend his ways and purify his heart. He denounced caste most emphatically and established the equality of man before God, "Who only wanted the purity of thought and action in human beings in order to favour them with salvation."

Caste and birth are not enquired, go and ask the Saints!
That's the caste and that descent, which is defined by deeds.[80]

What can the caste do ? Ascertain Truth."[81]

"Value the light within, don't ask about caste, for there is no caste hereafter."[82]

"Just as the grand idea of the Incomprehensible Unity, which could only be named and adored, levelled all distinctions of creed and caste, so did the great truth of the Brotherhood

---

79 Sir C. Gough
80 Rag Parbhatee, M. 1, Sh 6
ਜਾਤ ਜਨਮ ਨ ਪੂਛੀਐ, ਸਚ ਘਰ ਲੇਹੁ ਬਤਾਇ!
ਸਾ ਜਾਤ ਸ ਪਤ ਹੈ, ਜੇਹੇ ਕਰਮ ਕਮਾਇ॥
81 Var Majh, M. 1, Pauri 9.
ਜਾਤੀ ਦੇ ਕਿਆ ਹਥ ? ਸਚ ਪਰਖੀਐ।
82 Rag Asa, M. 1, Sh 3.
ਜਾਣੇ ਜੈਤ, ਨ ਪੂਛਹੁ ਜਾਤੀ, ਅਗੇ ਜਾਤ ਨ ਹੇ।

of man sweep away the barriers of nation, tribe and station. Nanak taught that all men are equal before God; that there is no high, no low, no dark, no fair, no privileged, no out-caste; all are equal both in race and in creed, in political rights and in religious aspiration.[83]

Dr. Trump remarks that the institution of caste was not directly assailed by Nanak, but, immediately after this remark, he quoted the last-mentioned *shabd* of the *Asa Rag* and goes on to say that "emancipation is not confined to the higher castes, but made accessible to all men, even to the *chandal*. Different stories are therefore cited in the *Granth* that even the lowest men attained to the salvation by muttering the name (of God).[84] Nanak received all men as his disciples without any regard to caste, recognising in all the dignity of human birth and thus laid the foundation of a popular religion." This shows that Dr. Trump's first lines were probably written in haste and without a full consideration of what was to follow or of what the real thing was. He has, in fact, in more than one place, expressed contradictory views, and, laudable though his attempt of translating *Guru Granth Sahib* was, his hasty conclusions and unwarranted opinions point to his scanty information and want of keen insight and, therefore, are deeply to be regretted.

"These two ideas, the Unity of God and the Brotherhood of man," says Pincot, "while uniting all classes on a common basis, at the same time, separated those who accepted them from the rest of their countrymen as an association of God-fearing republicans; for what Nanak claimed was *Liberty from prescribed trammels, Equality before God, and the Fraternity of Mankind.* The practical application of the doctrines thus taught led to the formation of a new nationality, the disciples of the great teacher becoming a republican fraternity, which gradually consolidated into a separate nation by the necessity for struggling for the liberty they claimed." Thus unity of God

83 Fredric Pincot.
84 This question will be explained and discuss presently.

and unity of mankind were the two fundamental doctrines of Guru Nanak. "Unison is the word," says Isaac Taylor, "which characterised true religion and describes the upper world." This was Guru Nanak's religion and this he preached to his followers. "Oneness," both of God and of mankind, was his motto, and he preached that whereas God is One, it will be the principal source of eternal beatitude for all brethren (*Bhais*, Sikhs) to dwell together in perfect unity. As God Himself is One, so is He pleased with Oneness. Produce concord and avoid discord; love all, despise none and produce Oneness; believe in One, love One, and Oneness, and be One.

Next to the above fundamental principles come the means of man's salvation. But, before proceeding to explain the means of salvation in Guru Nanak's religion, it seems necessary to know what constituted salvation, as taught by Guru Nanak. It has already been remarked that Guru Nanak did nowhere enter upon metaphysical or philosophical discussions, and that, in interpreting his teachings we are to keep all subtleties of the Hindu philosophy out of our consideration, and must put only popular construction upon the words used by him. That Guru Nanak believed in the transmigration of souls, is doubtless true.[85] He did teach of a previous birth and did connect the present with the deeds of the past. The present life is sure to be followed by another, whose nature will be determined by our own good and bad actions. This apprehension of a future birth is what troubles the soul of a man, and thus it is to get rid of this *apprehension*, which is a source of happiness to the soul.

No man but is striving hard to be happy. The attainment of everlasting happiness, the end which every man is trying to achieve, is what Nanak believed to be the salvation. In what form that eternal beatitude is attained is not discussed anywhere. But Nanak did teach that it could be reached, even in this life,

---

85 "Life is like the wheel circling on its pivot.
    O Nanak ! of going and coming there is no end.

and consisted of living *with* God and in God.[86] "Rare are such holy men," says Nanak, "in whose pure hearts lives the True one; seek the Lord's protection, and let the element meet the Principal Element."[87] One enjoys eternal happiness when God is constantly *with* him: and in which form he himself would then be, Guru Nanak has not cared much to discuss.

Those are saved, says Nanak, with whom the Father is pleased, on whom He bestow his favours'. "He, whom God favours, O Nanak find the Lord." Then are shown the ways in which the Lord may be pleased by man, methods by the employment of which His favours are won. "Yet the extension of grace," says Cunnningham, "is linked with the exercise of our will and the beneficent use of our faculties. God, says Nanak, places salvation in good works and uprightness of conduct; the Lord will ask of man, 'What has he done,' and the teacher further required timely repentance of men, saying, ' if not untill the day of reckoning the sinner abaseth himself, punishment shall overtake him'." Devotion of Him, meditation of His true name with a heart full of faith, and pure moral deeds, are the means by which the Grace of the Almighty is obtained; and these methods may be adopted by obeying the instruction given by the Guru. Thus implicit obedience to the Guru is shown to lead to man's salvation in the end. Some English writers have misunderstood the injunction to obey the Guru and have been led to the conclusion that the, "chief duty of the disciple is *blind* obedience of His Guru."[*88] An obedience to the instruction of the Guru with an ulterior object of one's own salvation, and even rendering manual service to such a mediator, is by no means a *blind* obedience to be so lightly and contemptuously treated. For "without the Guru love

---

86 Cunningham, however says that Nanak regarded bliss as the dwelling of the soul with God after its pituitary transmigration should have erased.
87 Rag Sorath M. 1, Gh 7 Sh 6.

ਸੂਚੇ ਭਾਂਡੇ ਸਾਚ ਸਮਾਵੈ ਵਿਰਲੈ ਸੁਚਾ ਚਾਰੀ।
ਤੱਤੇ ਕੋ ਪਰਮ ਤੱਤ ਮਿਲਾਇਆ, ਨਾਨਕ ਸਰਨ ਤੁਹਾਰੀ।

88 Dr. Trumph's *Adi Granth*, p. cx.

cannot be excited, (as without him) the filth of egoism cannot be removed."[89] It will be shown presently why such obedience is necessary to the attainment of eternal bliss by the disciple.

In the principle of *Bhakti* is included the unbounded love of God. Here is what Nanak himself says about that Love:-

O man! How will thou be released without Love ?
Through the Guru's Word, He becometh manifest as
      pervading all and exciteth Devotion in them?

O man, love God as the lotus loves the water!
The more it is beaten by the waves, the more its love is excited.

Having received its life in the water, it dies without water.

O man, love God as the fish loves the water!
The more the water is, the more is it joyous and its
      mind and body are contented.

Without water it cannot live for a moment,
      the pain of separation from water is so great to it.

O man, love God as *chatrik* loves the rain!
The tanks full and the lands green are nothing to it,
      without a single rain-drop.

O man, love god as the water loves the milk!
It endures itself the boiling, but doth not allow
      the milk to be consumed.

O man, love God as the *chakvi* loves the sun!
(Without sun) Doth not sleep for a moment, and
      considers as distant that which is present.[90]

---

89 Sri Rag, M. 1, Asht Sh. 11.
ਬਿਨ ਗੁਰ ਪ੍ਰੀਤ ਨ ਉਪਜੈ ਹਉਮੈ ਮੈਲ ਨ ਜਾਇ।
90 Sri Rag M.1, Asht, Sh, 11.
ਮਨ ਰੇ, ਕਿਉ ਛੂਟਹਿ ਬਿਨ ਪਿਆਰ ?

      THE CREED OF GURU NANAK

This principle of love is taken still further by Guru Nanak who likens the Deity to the husband and the disciple to the wife. Such a height of devotion and love can only be met with in the Indian systems and, perhaps, by far the most of all in the religion of Guru Nanak.

> All are the female friends of the Husband, all adorn themselves;
> They make their own estimates: but mind, fancy
>   dress is not the proper one,
> By hypocrisy the affection of the Husband is not
>   obtained; counterfeit overgilding is miserable.
> O God, thus the woman enjoys her husband!
> The favoured women, who please Thee, Thou
>   mercifully adoruest.
> The body and heart of her, who is adorned with the
>   Guru's Word, are with the Beloved(Husband);
> Both hands joined she stands and looks out and utters
>   an earnest prayer.
> She is steeped in colour of Devotion, dwells in fear of God

ਗੁਰਮੁਖਿ ਅੰਤਰਿ ਰਵਿ ਰਹਿਆ ਬਖਸੇ ਭਗਤ ਭੰਡਾਰ।
ਰੇ ਮਨ, ਐਸੀ ਹਰਿ ਸਿਉ ਪ੍ਰੀਤ ਕਰਿ ਜੈਸੀ ਜਲ ਕਮਲੇਹਿ;
ਲਹਰੀ ਨਾਲਿ ਪਛਾੜੀਐ ਭੀ ਵਿਗਸੈ ਅਸਨੇਹਿ;
ਜਲ ਮਹਿ ਜੀਅ ਉਪਾਏ ਕੈ ਬਿਨ ਜਲ ਮਰਣੁ ਤਿਨੇਹਿ।
ਰੇ ਮਨ, ਐਸੀ ਹਰਿ ਸਿਉ ਪ੍ਰੀਤ ਕਰਿ ਜੈਸੀ ਮਛਲੀ ਨੀਰ;
ਜੀਉ ਅਧਿਕਉ ਤਿਉ ਸੁਖੁ ਘਣੋ ਮਨਿ ਤਨਿ ਸ਼ਾਂਤਿ ਸਰੀਰ;
ਬਿਨੁ ਜਲ ਘੜੀ ਨ ਜੀਵਈ ਪ੍ਰਭ ਜਾਨੈ ਅਬ ਪੀਰ।
ਰੇ ਮਨ, ਐਸੀ ਹਰਿ ਸਿਉ ਪ੍ਰੀਤ ਕਰਿ ਜੈਸੀ ਚਾਤ੍ਰਿਕ ਮੇਹ;
ਸਰ ਭਰਿ ਥਲ ਹਰੀਆਵਲੇ ਇਕ ਬੂੰਦ ਨ ਪਵਈ ਕੇਹ।
*****

ਰੇ ਮਨ, ਐਸੀ ਹਰਿ ਸਿਉ ਪ੍ਰੀਤ ਕਰਿ ਜੈਸੀ ਜਲ ਦੁਧ ਹੋਇ;
ਆਵਟਣੁ ਆਪੇ ਖਵੇ ਦੁਧ ਕਉ ਖਪਣਿ ਨ ਦੇਹ।
*****

ਰੇ ਮਨ, ਐਸੀ ਹਰਿ ਸਿਉ ਪ੍ਰੀਤ ਕਰਿ ਜੈਸੀ ਚਕਵੀ ਸੂਰ;
ਖਿਨ ਪਲ ਨੀਦ ਨ ਸੋਵਈ ਜਾਨੈ ਦੂਰ ਹਜੂਰ॥

(her husband), she is steeped in the true colour of Love.
She shall not be widow who is absorbed in the True One,
    Her Husband is ever delightful, young, true, neither
dies nor departs.
He always sports with the beloved woman, true is
    His favourable look and good will towards her.

*****

She is beautiful among women, on those whose forehead
    is the Jewel of Love.

Her beauty and wisdom is charming by the infinite
    love of the True One.

Without her Beloved she knows no man, such is her
    love and affection for the True One.

O thou, who hast fallen asleep in the dark night,
    how will thy night pass without thy friend?

Thy bosom burns, thy body is set on fire, thy heart too,
    O lady, is being consumed?

When the woman is not enjoyed by Her Husband,
    her youth passes away to no purpose.

On the bed is the Husband, but the wife hath
    fallen to sleep and knoweth (Him) not.

I have fallen asleep, my Beloved is waking, whom
    else shall I ask about Him.

Whosoever fears Him, him the True Guru unites;,
    Love says Nanak, is her true companion,[91].

---

91 Sri Rag. M. 1, Asht, Sh. 2
ਸਭੇ ਕੰਤ ਮਹੇਲੀਆਂ ਸਗਲੀਆਂ ਕਰਹਿ ਸੀਗਾਰ,

THE CREED OF GURU NANAK

What sort of lovers are those who go after others?
Those are the chosen lovers who are ever absorbed.
Those to whom good is good and evil evil,
And who thus make calculations, are not the proper lovers.[92]

Wanted thou to play in Love?
Hand in hand, come into my street.

ਗਣਤ ਗਣਾਵਣ ਆਂਈਆ ਸੂਹਾ ਵੇਸੁ ਵਿਕਾਰ,
ਪਾਖੰਡ ਪ੍ਰੇਮੇ ਨ ਪਾਈਐ ਖੋਟਾ ਪਾਜ ਖੁਆਰ।
ਹਰਿ ਜੀ ਇਉ ਪਿਰ ਰਾਵੈ ਨਾਰਿ,
ਤੁਧ ਭਾਵਨ ਸੋਹਾਗਣੀ ਆਪਣੀ ਕਿਰਪਾ ਲੈਹਿ ਸਵਾਰ
ਗੁਰ ਸਬਦੀ ਸੀਗਾਰੀਆ ਤਨ ਮਨ ਪਿਰ ਕੈ ਪਾਸਿ,
ਦੋਇ ਕਰ ਜੋੜ ਖੜੀ ਤਕੈ ਸਚ ਕਹੇ ਅਰਦਾਸਿ।
ਲਾਲ ਰਤੀ ਸਚ ਭੈ ਵਸੀ ਭਾਇ ਰਤੀ ਰੰਗ ਰਾਸਿ।
ਸਾਧਨ ਰੰਡ ਨ ਬੈਸਈ ਜੇ ਸਤਿ ਗੁਰ ਮਾਹੀ ਸਮਾਇ,
ਪਿਰ ਰੀਸਾਲੂ ਨਉਤਨੇ ਸਾਚਉ ਮਰੈ ਨ ਜਾਇ,
ਨਿਤ ਰਵੈ ਸੋਹਾਗਣੀ ਸਚੀ ਨਦਰ ਰਜਾਇ।
                    *****
ਨਾਰੀ ਅੰਦਰ ਸੋਹਣੀ ਮਸਤਕ ਮਣੀ ਪਿਆਰੁ,
ਸੋਭਾ ਸੁਰਤਿ ਸੁਹਾਵਣੀ ਸਾਚੇ ਪ੍ਰੇਮਿ ਅਪਾਰ,
ਬਿਨ ਪਿਰ ਪੁਰਖ ਨ ਜਾਣਈ ਸਾਰੈ ਗੁਰ ਕੈ ਹੇਤਿ ਪਿਆਰਿ
ਨਿਸ ਅੰਧਿਆਰੀ ਸੁਤੀਐ ਕਿਉ ਪਿਰ ਬਿਨੁ ਰੈਣਿ ਵਿਹਾਇ
ਅੰਕ ਜਲਉ ਤਨ ਜਾਲੀਓ ਮਨ ਤਨ ਜਲਿ ਬਲਿ ਜਾਇ,
ਜਾ ਧਨ ਕੰਤ ਮਹੇਲੜੀ ਸੁਤੀ ਬੁਝ ਨ ਪਾਇ,
ਹਉ ਸੁਤੀ ਪਿਰ ਜਾਗਣਾ ਕਿਸ ਕਉ ਪੂਛਉ ਜਾਇ,
ਸਤਿ ਗੁਰਿ ਮੇਲੀ ਭੈ ਵਸੀ ਨਾਨਕ ਪ੍ਰੇਮੁ ਸਖਾਇ,
92 Asa di *var shlok* 20.
ਏ ਕਿਨੇਹੀ ਆਸਕੀ ਦੂਜੇ ਲਗੈ ਜਾਇ,
ਨਾਨਕ ਆਸਕੁ ਕਾਢੀਐ ਸਦ ਹੀ ਰਹੈ ਸਮਾਇ।
ਚੰਗੇ ਚੰਗਾ ਕਰਿ ਮੰਨੇ ਮੰਦੈ ਮੰਦਾ ਹੋਇ,
ਆਸਕੁ ਏਹ ਨ ਆਖੀਐ ਜਿ ਲਖੈ ਵਰਤੈ ਸੋਇ।

Sacrifice thy head (life), waver not;
Then alone step forth into this path.[93]

Thus it would appear that the principle of Love has been taken to the highest pitch by Guru Nanak. He was by far the greatest preacher of this principle, and love taken out of his religion, the whole fabric must necessarily fall to the ground. The whole system of Guru Nanak is founded on Love. Brotherhood and equality of man is one of the two fundamental principles of his creed, as stated above. In other words, Love for humanity was his religion; so too unbounded Love for God was the principal means of salvation.

Then comes the meditation of God's name with a sincere heart, - "muttering of God's name," as Dr. Trump has so slightingly translated the term. "Muttering," though not literally an incorrect translation of the word *japna,* does not express the correct meaning of it. *Japna, simrna, dhyana, smana,* muttering, remembering, meditating, absorbing are all used synonymously by Guru Nanak, and the most rational, reasonable and popular interpretation of it is that God should ever *dwell* in the disciple's heart: He should *never be forgotten.* "When rising, when sitting, when sleeping, and when waking, ever and always think of Hari." It means that man should *always* be God-acknowledging, God-fearing, God-loving and God-knowing.[94]

The efficacy of prayer and also the forgiveness of past sins by the Grace of God are also the principles which are acknowledged by Guru Nanak. Prayer must ascend from the

---

93 *Shlok*, M. 1 sh 20.
ਜੇ ਤੇਨੁ ਪ੍ਰੇਮ ਖੇਲਨ ਕਾ ਚਾਇ,
ਸਿਰ ਧਰਿ ਤਲੀ ਗਲੀ ਮੇਰੀ ਆਇ।
ਸਿਰ ਦੀਜੈ ਕਾਣ ਨ ਕੀਜੇ,
ਤਉ ਇਸ ਮਾਰਗ ਪਾਉ ਧਰੀਜੇ।।
94 "Eat and clothe thyself and thou may eat be happy ; but without fear and faith(Love) there is no salvation". Sohilla Maroo Rag.

THE CREED OF GURU NANAK

sincere and humble heart of man to God and it is sure to be heard. "As a large ocean is full of water, so are my sins, O God! Be kind and be graceful. Thou hast raised sunk stones to the surface!"[95] "Born in sins, committing sins, and always living in sins: Cannot be purified by washing, let us wash a hundred times. If He forgives, we shall be forgiven, says Nanak, otherwise they (sins) shall go on accumulating."[96]

The last, but not the least of all are the pure moral deeds. Without purity of life, neither of the above means of salvation are attainable by man. Pure moral deeds are, so to say, the means to the means of salvation. And how far Guru Nanak insisted upon purity of life may well be verified by a reference to any chapter of this volume. It seems quite needless to detain the reader in dilating upon the details of the moral duties on which Guru Nanak insisted, for Morality of Sikhism is a subject well worthy of a separate volume which, it is hoped, some abler hand would, sooner or later, deal with. The remarks of Dr. Trump that "in a religion, where the highest object of life is the extinction of individual existence, there can be no room for a system of moral duties," and his assumption that "Sikhism is not a moralizing Deism," carry their own refutation with them, and the readers of this volume need not be reminded how absurd this notion of the German Translator is.

In the conclusion of this chapter, it may once more be pointed out that it is here that the company of Saints and holy men and obedience to the instruction of Guru are most useful for a Sikh. The moral tone of a man's character can never be high unless he scrupulously abstains from bad company, and seeks

---

95 Rag Gowree, M. 1, Sh 17.

ਜੇਤਾ ਸਮੁੰਦ ਸਾਗਰ ਨੀਰ ਭਰਿਆ ਤੇਤੇ ਅੰਗਨ ਹਮਾਰੇ।
ਦਇਆ ਕਰਹੁ ਕਿਛੁ ਮਿਹਰ ਉਪਾਵਹੁ ਡੁਬਦੇ ਪਾਥਰ ਤਾਰੇ।

96 *Var Majh*, M. 1 *Shlok* 23.

ਖਤਿਅਹੁ ਜੰਮੇ, ਖਤੇ ਕਰ ਨਿਤਿ ਖਤਿਆ ਵਿਚੁ ਪਾਹਿ।
ਧੋਤੇ ਮੂਲ ਨ ਉਤਰਹਿ ਜੇ ਸਉ ਧੋਵਣ ਪਾਹਿ।
ਨਾਨਕ, ਬਖਸੇ ਬਖਸੀਅਹਿ, ਨਾਹਿ ਤਾ ਪਾਹੀ ਪਾਹਿ।

frequents the company of Saints and other good men. In order
to be good and noble, man must always keep before his eyes a
high ideal if virtue and devotion. Well does Guru Nanak say:

> Whoever tells me of Thee, my Master, what shall I present
> him with?
> I shall cut my head and offer it to him for a seat and without
> head serve him.
> Why should I not die and give life (for him)? For it is the
> Lord who is so respected in him.[97]

ॐ

---

97 Rag Vadihana, M.1, gh2, sh 3.
ਤੇ ਸਾਹਿਬੁ ਕੀ ਬਾਤ ਜਿ ਆਖੈ ਕਹੁ ਨਾਨਕ ਤਿਸ ਕਿਆ ਦੀਜੈ॥
ਸੀਸ ਵਢੇ ਕਰਿ ਬੈਸਣ ਦੀਜੈ ਵਿਣ ਸਿਰ ਸੇਵ ਕਰੀਜੈ।
ਕਿਉ ਨ ਮਰੀਜੈ ਜੀਅੜਾ ਨ ਦੀਜੈ ਜਾ ਸਹੁ ਭਇਆ ਵਿਡਾਣਾ॥

CHAPTER 10
THE CHURCH OF GURU NANAK

" Prophets sent come into this world, but when He so pleases, they are sent for, bound hand and foot". This is what Guru Nanak believed about the missions of the great Reformers of this world, himself included. The same seems to have been the notion of all reformers who passed before him, though not expressed in words, yet clearly indicated by their actions. They knew that their life was quite uncertain. The task that was imposed upon them was hard and it was their duty to do it efficiently with the aid of as many suitable assistants as they could possibly secure. The work of Reformation is not of a single day or a single year, or even of a single century. These movements must even remain astir on this earth, otherwise mankind is apt to fall back from it, if left alone. Nor could its range be confined to a single town, province or country. It must cover a wide area or it must die its natural death. It is thus true that the great Reformers had to set up their churches. Christ had to tain twelve disciples whom he sent abroad to preach his gospel in distant lands, and Muhammad had to train his followers to spread the awe of his scimetar throughout the length of this hemisphere. The great Buddha himself established monasteries and churches in different parts

92

of Asia to teach people to be honest and good. So also, it would appear, did Guru Nanak, in setting up *Manjis* in different parts of Southern Asia, provide for the continuance of his Mission after his departure. These *Manjis* were in fact the District Churches established by Guru Nanak where his followers were ordered to assemble to hear the instructions given by the head of the Church. As already pointed out, the word *Manji* means a cot and these churches were so called because the head of the church used to sit on a cot while the audience used to squat on the floor. Around this *Manji* used to assemble the Sikhs of the village, town or district, daily or occasionally to hear what their leader had to tell them concerning their duties, religious, social and moral. These early Sikhs though few in number, were very zealous and sincere, and their congregations were really examples of an assembly of sincere and pious enthusiasts. Mutual confidence and mutual faith were the foremost features of these meetings. Ready to serve and obey his leader, every Sikh of such congregation was a model of humility, determination and strong faith. For had not the founder of their sect enjoined them to serve and obey the leader, as they would serve and obey him, and had he not told them that humble though every Sikh should be, he should also be strong of determination and faith. He had also told them in his address to Mardana, "O Mardana! The world is foolish and will turn to after thee after groveling in the dust for ages." Were not these words sufficient to inspire them with strong hopes and high aspirations?

Such then were the churches founded by Guru Nanak. Each individual Sikh was entitled *Bhai*, Brother and collectively, the habitations or congregations of Sikhs were called *Sangats*, where one of them "always presided over the rest."

Guru Nanak founded these *Manjis* by himself first appointing one of his Sikhs to preside over each *Sangat*. Whether Guru Nanak himself gave him the title of *Baba*, it is not quite sure, but there is no doubt in this that the title of Father, *Baba*, was found being used regarding them immediately after Guru Nanak. The probability, however, is that it was also instituted by Guru Nanak, whose sons, Sri Chand and Lakhmi Chand, seems to have got the title as an honorary distinction. Above these *Babas,* as the head of the entire Church, was the Guru himself. The lowest order being that of *Bhais*, every Sikh had an inherent right to this order. In fact, all Sikhs are brothers-in-Guru, and therefore is Sikhism invariably called a Brotherhood or Fraternity. The next higher order was that of *Babas* or Fathers, who were generally put in charge of *Manjis* where they used to teach the Brotherhood under them. The Brotherhood had to pay no tax to the *Baba*. The latter generally worked himself for his bread and earned a living for himself and his family, just as any other Sikh did. In most cases his own house was the place of congregational meetings, for it was there that he was seated on a *Manji*. His superiority lay only in his purer heart and morals, in his being attached to the person of Guru Nanak, and in his having won his personal favour. No limit seems to have been put on the number of *Babas*. Besides denoting the occupation of the office of the head of a church, it also seems to have been an honorary distinction, to be bestowed on deserving candidates. The highest of these orders was that of the *Guru* (the Great Teacher), and this title and the office pertaining thereto was to be held by only one man in the whole Church. He was the Head of the entire Brotherhood, and all others were to obey his precepts and teachings, and it was under his orders that they had the power to convert others. All power and all instruction emanated from him, and he was to be ordered by none. He alone could raise *Bhai*s to the order of *Babas,* and none else but he could raise a *Bhai* or a *Baba* to be *Guru* after him.

All these orders seem to have been bestowed for life, as the hearts once converted were presumed to have changed for life. The higher orders were not bestowed until a very long and thorough trial proved beyond the possibility of a doubt that the candidate is no longer liable to fall back from it. But it should nevertheless be remembered that should such an unfortunate event ever happen, no hesitation was made to degrade him.

Neither were these orders hereditary. Although the son generally follows the faith of his father, yet it is not necessarily and universally so, and still less are the chances of his being equally pure, noble, faithful, and devoted with his father. But should the son *be* his father's equal, there was no *bar* to his attaining to the same position. Age was no consideration in the bestowal of these orders, nor was the length of service or period of conversation any criterion for that. It was what the candidate had proved himself to be, in however short period it may be, that was the chief consideration with the Guru.

That Guru Nanak himself was also a member of the Brotherhood he had formed cannot be doubted. That he had a superiority over all others in as much as he was the Founder of the Fraternity is also true. But that he did not mean it to be understood, that he was high and above all others so much that he could not be reached by the members of the lower orders who had simply to look up to and admire him, without attempting to follow his example, which unconscious feeling was being entertained for him, will also be clear from the ceremony of the transfer of the charge of his office which he performed before his ascension. The fact that he seated his successor on the chief *Manji,* and laying certain presents before him, he, along with his followers, bowed down before him, clearly indicates that he wanted to impress his followers that he himself was also one of the Brotherhood of the Sikhs, and that his superiority lay only in the work that he had performed, and that henceforth no particular individual was to be worshipped all being of the same class. The high seat on the chief *Manji,* to which, of course, all respect and reverence was due, as it entailed very heavy duties and responsibilities on its occupier, was within the reach of every Sikh. From ordinary ranks one could rise to that exalted position and to that ranks would he return after making over its charge to his successor. By reverting to the ranks before his ascension, Guru Nanak, in fact raised, to a very great extent, the lower orders. Now at least could his followers see seated along with themselves, below the chief *Manji*, one who had given them their religion, telling them, that he was only one of themselves, and here also they could see one of themselves lifted to the exalted position of Guru, inspiring them with high aspirations.

It is nevertheless to be noted that though Guru Nanak by this last action of his took away from the office of the Guru the reverential awe that it had gradually inspired in others, yet the reverence and love for the occupier of it, which were perhaps purposely left to subsist, gradually and unconsciously developed into man-worship, in the end, required the energy and sagacity of no less a person than Guru Govind Singh to put a stop to.

One thing more concerning these orders must be mentioned before leaving this subject. The entrance into the Brotherhood of the Sikhs did not require abandonment of household duties. On the other hand, "Nanak also taught that the position of the householder, as head of the family and engaged in the business of the world, was most honorable,[98] and he strongly discouraged the idea that any special virtue was to be gained by the ascetic life. That true religion consisted not in outward ceremonial and the acceptance of the religious profession but in the state of the heart and that it was possible to meditate with advantage on spiritual things while engaged in the ordinary business of life without retreating to the wilderness or the seclusion of a monastery. It is true that several ascetic bodies of Sikhs, of whom the *Udasis* and *Akalis*[99] are the most numerous,

---

98 A householder who does no evil, who is even intent upon good, who continuously do charity, such a householder is pure as Ganges.

Ramkullee Rarjnee.

Householder and hornets are equal, whoever meditates on the name of the Lord.

Assa Rarjnee.

99 The *Akalis*, however are not prohibited to marry. Their unsettled life has no doubt accustomed them not to marry and beget families but should

subsequently broke away from the teaching of the Nanak, but these have always been considered, more or less, unorthodox, and the Sikh religion, as taught both by Nanak and Govind Singh, was eminently suited for practical life."[100]

In conclusion of this chapter it is necessary to note that a baptismal rite also seems to have been instituted by Guru Nanak to initiate a candidate into the Sikh Fraternity. Sir Lepel Griffin says that the "old Sikh faith had a baptismal rite which had fallen into disuse. This was resuscitated by Govind Singh, as the necessary initiatory ceremony of Sikhism." With this last proposition it is difficult to agree. Keeping in view the fact that Guru Nanak was not at all a man of conventions, the ceremony instituted by him could not possibly have been of a military character which is the characteristic of that which was introduced by Guru Govind Singh and is prevalent now. What that ceremony was is also difficult to say. But it seems that it was of the nature of *charan-ghal*, washing of the feet of the Guru, because even up to this day, we, though not now so generally on account of the Radical movement of the societies, called Singh Sabhas, yet occasionally, see the descendants of Guru Nanak claiming to be Gurus themselves, administer the washing of their right toe to the candidates entering their following. It is not improbable that this ceremony of theirs is merely a remnant of the old Sikh baptismal rite, referred to above.

CRQZO

they do so, as a good number of them may have seen with families, they are not looked down by the other member of their body. On the other hand such of their members are respected as having truly followed the precept of (Guru Govind Singh, implies in words ਔਰਤ ਈਮਾਨ (Wife is piety) Another seet of nirmalas, however, forma purely ascetic body.
100   Sir Lepel Griffin

THE CHURCH OF GURU NANAK

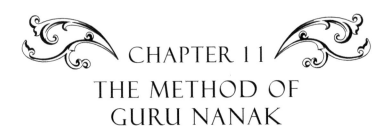

CHAPTER 11
THE METHOD OF GURU NANAK

Guru Nanak had a method of teaching peculiar to himself. He taught not by speculating about God by lengthy arguments or illustrative parables, like a school professor, drawing out conclusions by laying down logical premises, but chiefly by example and authority. He exemplified upon himself all the doctrines which he taught and in his person his followers found not only a divine preceptor but also an exemplar of the principles which he preached. Himself safe from the attacks of his fault-finding adversaries, he preached with an authority which seemed natural with him. He does not argue at any length but he commands. He is not afraid of adversaries and does not depend much upon the assistance of his friends. He has confidence in himself, and is certain that his words cannot be lost in vain. He simply speaks of God and spiritual things as one who has come out from Him, to tell us what he knows, and his simple telling brings us the reality.

Example is better than precept. Himself a non-believer of the outer formalities, Guru Nanak takes the first opportunity of showing the absurdity and the superstitious character of *Yagyopwit* (the sacred thread of the Hindus) when it was going to be administered to himself in his early years. On *Sutak* (the birth ceremony of the Hindus, which also has a superstitious character about it) he does not express his views till the birth of his first son gives an occasion to do so. Similarly he waits to acquit himself on the Hindu death-ceremonies till his own last moments, when he makes a sort of will as to what ought to be the ceremonies to be performed after his departure. But on all of these occasion he does not want to destroy altogether all traces of those principles. He does not offend anybody merely by denouncing their popular beliefs through and through. Even and anon, he wants to replace those popular beliefs and prejudices by a higher and nobler doctrine. While showing the useless character of the *Yagyopwit*, he asks the Brahman to wear and administer the spiritual thread which he describes. While exposing the vain character of Muhammadan form of worship, he tells the *Mullah* and Kazi to acquire the noble, pure and spiritual qualities in order to be true Mussalmans. Neither the Brahman nor the *Mullah* could, under these circumstances, differ from him and all at once bow to him in obeisance and humility. They get conquered but do not feel any mortification. On the other hand, they get attached to his person. While in Mecca, he does not mean to tell the priest and pilgrims that *Kaaba* was not the house of God but he tells them that God's house was on all sides. While at Jaggannath he does not threaten the group of worshippers with punishment for their idol-worship, but he tells them to worship the real Thakurji (the Lord) in their spirit, ever and always, and, for that purpose, to lay down their present *Arti* aside and to make one of different materials which can in no case fail them. He ask the hearers to think of the grandeur of the Universe and then to admire, and pray, to the Creator of all those things. Similarly in Brindaban and other places. It will thus be seen that the very method of Guru Nanak's teaching was calculated to make room for him in people's hearts, as much as the purity of his doctrine and the sublimity of his character.

His way of announcing his arrival at a place in order to attract attention was also a novel one, as must have been noticed in the foregoing pages. As soon as he arrives at a certain place and notices some objectionable popular prejudices and practices, he places himself at once in a position openly antagonistic to those practices in order to attract special attention. For instance, at Kurukshetra he cooks meat in a public place, when Hindus assembled here at the festival of *Surya grihin* (eclipse Of the Sun) were performing *tarpan* (ceremony of water-giving). The Brahmans and others get indignant at this outrage, news spread like fire throughout the *mela*, people come upon him furiously, when, after briefly explaining his conduct, he delivers a beautiful sermon on the wrong ways of the world in their search after truth. He does not tell them that they were doomed or that they were going after a wrong end, but taking for granted their innocence and sincerity, he tells them that they were following a wrong path which would not lead then to *their desired destination.*

At Hardwar, he begins to throw water to the west when people assembled there at a great *Kumbhi mela* were offering handful of water to their ancestors and to the Sun to the east. People laugh at him, a fairly large crowd gather round him and question him about his object in doing so, when he tells them that he was watering his crops at Kartarpore some 300 miles away in the west. On a still louder laughter from the crowd over this, he begins to expose the absurdity of their whole ceremony. Then he goes on to tell them the true principles of religion and the means of salvation. At Jaggannath, he attracts public notice by keeping sitting posture at the time of the *Arti* ceremony to the idols in the temple. Similarly at Mecca he advertises his arrival by lying down with his feet towards the *Kaaba.*

In an age when there was no printing presses and no public notice-boards. and when neither were any other means available to gather an audience, no better method could be adopted for the purpose than the one he followed. This method had the advantage at once of notifying his arrival and of introducing a subject for discussion. Once attracting an audience in this manner, his divine abilities and holy and spiritual life afterwards charmed those present to come daily and hear his sermons regularly.

ଓଃ୪ଠ

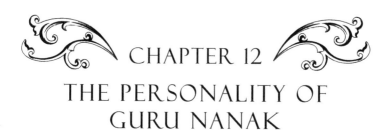

CHAPTER 12

THE PERSONALITY OF GURU NANAK

To understand the personality of Guru Nanak is by no means an easy task, and yet the task is not a very difficult one for a sincere investigator. In fact the character of Guru Nanak presents to the student of his life a strange combination of qualities. A number of paradoxes, more apparent than real, seem to strike the imagination of the student of his character, and our timid methods of investigation do not afford us a sufficiency of historical explanations. Guru Nanak lived at a time when the game of public life was freely played, during a period of human activity when man risks all and gains all. The movement which he started implies Liberty, and opposed by the combined forces of his adversaries, people who could not cherish to be told that they were degraded, those who did not like to be raised from their low level, the apotheosis was reached, when Guru Nanak was incarcerated in jail, when he was himself deprived of at least the physical part of the very liberty which he was preaching. But who could deprive him of the liberty of conscience, the liberty of thought and the liberty of action which were his natural gifts and which he did not fail to exercise even in the most adverse circumstances. Genial and frank, with an unlimited capacity for reform, he made troops of followers wherever he went. Nanak was "thorough and consistent, prudent and yet urgent, and as gentle in manner as he was strong in faith." The movement which he started was not the result of a long meditation and deep thought but had a spontaneous growth from the inborn nature of its great Founder. Guru Nanak had no dogma, but a fixed personal resolution which, exceeding in intensity every other created will, governs to this hour the destinies of millions of human souls.

For Guru Nanak, nature had dealt her choicest both in body and mind. Strong healthy physique, beautiful features and white rosy colour were the most prominent features of his body, and his physiognomy always impressed all who looked at him with his sacred character and inspired them with spontaneous reverence towards him. Men became his followers not by believing this thing or that thing, but by being attached to his person. He laughed very seldom, yet he never produced the impression of austerity, moroseness, sadness or unhappiness. He was, on the other hand, rejoicing in spirit. At times he was sarcastic but always serious. He was discontented with the world but had contentment within himself. His heart burnt within him at the degraded condition of his fellow-beings but he worked very prudently and ever successfully. With strong and forceful expression, straight-forward and bold demeanour, never allowing any opportunity to slip and ever ready to teach and reform, Guru Nanak presents a character thorough and consistent from the very beginning. In his character we do not find any improvements being made, for he was thorough in his childhood. Does not the young child of seven and nine present the similar spectacles at the school and at his *Yagyopwit* ceremony as were presented by the grown up Guru Nanak at Kurukshetra, Hardwar, Brindaban and Jaggannath, and is not the incident of crops of his ninth year quite consistent with one of Bawa Wali at Hassanabadal? The trait of his character which has been misunderstood by many to be the habit of extravagance and carelessness in money matters, and which seems to have led Mr. Fredric Pincot to remark that "his practice to give in alms to the poor all the material wealth which came into his possession, however, laudable it may have been, soon degenerated into an infatuation; and no property was safe if entrusted to young Nanak," has already been discussed. In fact he had no extravagances to prune off, no eccentricities to return from. His character is never *modified*, it is the one and the same throughout. Never hesitating in doing his task, never faltering in his trails, undaunted in adversity, unshaken amid persecution, Guru Nanak presents a character, thorough and consistent all round, and without a parallel in the history of the world.

Guru Nanak was a man among men. His example inspire us with hopes and aspirations. Nowhere does he say that he is beyond approach by mortal men. He raises his fellow-beings towards himself. He, infact, tells us, in actions as in words, that every human being is capable of being like him, only if one would like and try to be so. He does not leave us behind exhausted. Each step he draws us neared to himself and inspires us with fresher aspirations. His life and teachings do not mortify us, even far below in the lowest depth of degradation. His loving hand, on the other hand, seems to extend itself to us even there.

It has already been said that Guru Nanak had set up a new dispensation and founded the True Religion, in all its pristine glory and purity. So far as other religious systems were concerned, he follows none and denounced none. He was not a Hindu, yet he was the purest of Hindus; he was not a Mussalman, yet he was the holiest of Mussalmans. So with the other minor religious systems, which prevailed in India during his period, Christianity had not yet reached India, and we, therefore, do not find him anywhere referring to it. But, so far as the general tenor of his doctrine is considered, it may also be safely said that he was not a Christian, yet he was the noblest of all Christians. Guru Nanak's perfect idealism was the highest rule of unspotted and virtuous life. The foundation of True Religion was, indeed, his work. After him, all that remained was to develop it and make it fruitful. His great work, indeed, was to have made himself beloved, in the highest degree, by his disciples, and his doctrine was so little dogmatic that he never dreamed of writing or causing it to be written. His *shabds,* now found preserved in *Guru Granth Sahib,* were first written in scattered scraps by his disciples, as they heard them, and were collected immediately after him by his successor, Guru Angad, and were incorporated in *Guru Granth* by the Fifth Guru, Arjun Dev. He himself was thoroughly illiterate, for he could neither read or write, but his soul-stirring verses in his vernacular Punjabi indicate his spiritual inspirations and "are still read with fervour, and will long continue to be read with devotion and reverence." Guru Nanak claims to be an inspired teacher, in as much as he says that "as the word is received form the Lord, so do I give the knowledge thereof (to the world), O Lalo." This is not merely a pretension. His whole life indicates the one and only one inference that his teaching could not but be from above. His undaunted and bold behaviour, even under circumstances the most trying, and his lofty and sacred doctrines lead us to the same conclusion. Then, there is the fact that, for about four hundred years past, the Sikhs have believed and do now believe his sayings to be inspired, so much so that his teachings have always been inspiring and will ever inspire fresher spirit and zeal in the breasts of his followers. It will thus be understood how pure Sikhism, the product of a perfectly spontaneous spiritual movement, freed from its birth from all dogmatic restraint, having struggled for four hundred years of liberty of conscience, despite its failures, still reaps the fruits of its glorious origin. To renew itself it has but to return to *Guru Granth Sahib.*

This sublime being we may call divine, not in the sense that he has absorbed all divinity, or has been identical with it, but in the sense that Nanak is he who has caused his fellowmen to make the greatest step towards the divine. Guru Nanak, in fact, created heaven, upon this very earth, of pure souls, and, to find its essential characteristics, one may well refer to the state of his disciples in his time and immediately after it. In Guru Nanak, whom we may well describe as a man among men and a god among gods, was concentrated all that was good and lofty in human nature. Infallible he was not. But he conquered all those passions which we fight against. Never has any man, so much as he, made the interests of humanity predominate in his life over the pettiness of self-love. Unreservedly bound to his mission, he subordinated all things to it, and it was by the intensity of this heroic will that he conquered heaven. The legend of Guru Nanak's life will always bring into activity all the tender feelings of human soul, and all ages will proclaim that amongst the sons of man few were born greater than Nanak.

> Yes, write it in the rock..............
> Grave it on brass with adamantine pen!
> 'Tis God Himself becomes apparent, when
> God's wisdom and God's goodness are displayed,
> For God of these His attributes is made.

Mathew Arnold.

ॐ

Lightning Source UK Ltd.
Milton Keynes UK
UKHW021101110520
363093UK00007B/931